M000237415

SECRETS LEARNED I

DEAD
FOR 34
MINUTES

A TRUE STORY OF LIFE AFTER DEATH

Never give up!
Senator Mike Crotts

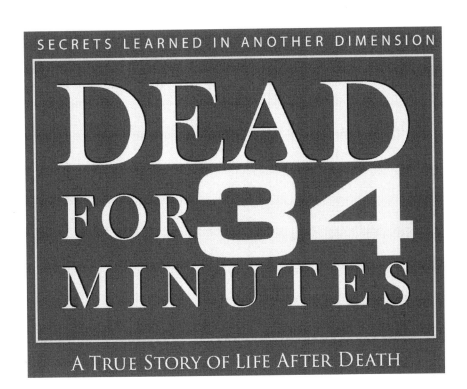

SECRETS LEARNED IN ANOTHER DIMENSION

DEAD FOR 34 MINUTES

A TRUE STORY OF LIFE AFTER DEATH

Former Senator Mike Crotts

Copyright © 2018 Mike D. Crotts

Dead For 34 Minute
A True Story of Life After Death

Editor: Robert Rivera: rrivera942@gmail.com
Editor: Gail Zapf: mikecrotts.com

Book Cover Design: Abner Ramos; ramosabner77@gmail.com

Printed in the USA

ISBN 978-0-692-17555-2

All Rights Reserved. This book is protected by the copyright laws of the United States of America. This book may not be copied or reprinted for commercial gain or profit. The use of short quotations is permitted. Permission will be granted upon request. The author guarantees all contents are original and do not infringe upon the legal rights of any other person or work. Unless otherwise identified, Scripture quotations are from the New King James Version and The King James version. Used by permission. All rights reserved. Please note that Rising Starr Publications publishing style capitalizes certain pronouns in Scripture and out of Scripture that refer to God, Father, Son, His, and Holy Spirit, and may differ from some publisher's styles. Take note that the name devil, satan and related names are not capitalized. We choose not to acknowledge him, even to the point of disregarding grammatical rules.

Prepared for Publication By

Rising Starr Publications

1096 Highway 20 E McDonough, GA. 30252

First Edition

For book information or to write to the author:
www.mikecrotts.com

DEDICATION

In loving memory of Prophet Kim Clement. A man of great character with the highest standards of integrity, honesty, and loyalty. He championed many causes over his lifetime; never allowing the prevailing opinion of man to divert him from the course that God had called him. He reached the unreachable, loved the unlovable, and touched the untouchable. His boundless enthusiasm and energy in completing every challenge that crossed his path, was a privilege to watch. Kim believed and practiced what he preached with his whole heart. He taught me so much about hearing from God. He especially taught me about understanding the difference in imperfect and perfect praise and how to worship God, which is really a lifestyle.

No one that I know will ever embody all his spiritual traits, his unique personality, or the magnitude of his generosity. Besides being a great man of God, he was my good friend, my confidant, and my brother in the faith. Kim's spirit will continue to live on through his beautiful family and all those who were touched by his ministry. We have not yet seen or heard all the words he prophesied come to pass ... but, we will.

We loved Kim Clement and will never forget him, nor will we ever stop trying to accomplish all God spoke to us through this amazing modern-day Prophet of God.

SPECIAL TRIBUTE

To my wife, Phyllis, whom I love and adore. Whose faith, love, and spiritual walk with God gave her the courage to call my spirit back into my body. It was her prayer, spiritual insight, agreement, and alignment with the Holy Spirit at the precise moment He said, *"Do it now; Call him back!"*

She is my rock, my best friend, and my inspiration. Her faith, love, dedication, and encouragement in my life has been the greatest gift that God could give to any man.

Her numerous hours of editing and writing abilities has enlightened every page. This book is as much hers as it is mine, I cannot thank her enough.

ENDORSEMENTS

"I've been waiting in breathless anticipation for this book for years. Senator Crotts is one of the few people I've personally interviewed who has been revived from the dead and given insight into things to come. Mike Crotts' story differs from others with testimonies about life after death in two ways. First, over and over he has explained to me that there were certain details he was not at liberty to reveal until he had permission from God to do so. Second, he always told me that there were certain details of his experience and conversation with the Holy Spirit that he could not recall until God brought it back to his memory. Needless to say, I cannot wait to see what parts of his testimony are revealed now in this book.

The presence of God comes upon the room whenever I talk about the miracle that Phyllis and Senator Crotts experienced and I believe the same

Spirit will be upon you as you read their remarkable story."

Author; CEO; Director; Dr. Lance Wallnau
Lance Learning Group Center for Faith & Diplomacy
Washington, D.C.

"This book will take you to a new place in your life. The transparency in which Senator Mike and Phyllis Crotts live and love is refreshing. They are two of the most genuinely selfless people I've ever met. Mike has a great gift of wisdom while Phyllis has a great gift of hearing from God in the prophetic. Whether it is touching the lives of thousands of children or serving God in the political arena, wherever they go they bring an atmosphere of hope. The actual events of their lives give us the example of how faith mixed with love really works."

Author; President; Bishop Duane Swilley
Duane Swilley Ministries
Miami, Florida

"We have had the privilege of knowing Senator Mike Crotts for over 20 years. He has served his community and the State of Georgia with integrity and passion. He has a dynamic testimony that God has used to encourage and convict many to believe in the miraculous. We are glad he is sharing his testimony in this book *Dead for Thirty-Four Minutes: A True Story of Life After Death.* It will challenge you but assure you of the greatness and generosity of our God. What a blessing! We believe this is the time God has chosen to bring these truths to light. Mike has lived and demonstrated a life of service to God, country, and family. We are both delighted to call him our friend and co-laborer in the Kingdom of God."

Founder; Dr. Mary Crum
President; Co-Founder; Dr. W. Paul "Buddy" Crum
Life Center Ministries
Atlanta, Georgia

ACKNOWLEDGEMENTS

To a real hero, my son, Caleb Dane (Cale) Crotts. I love him with all my heart and I am so thankful for the life saving skills he administered to me during two separate medical crises. I am alive today thanks to his prompt actions, training, and knowledge of what needed to be done to save my life. His remarkable quick-thinking efforts are an important part of the content and completion of this book.

To my parents, Margaret and Thurmon Crotts, whose love, sacrifices and guidance in my life knew no bounds. They both encouraged me to "write this book!" I love and miss them tremendously. My hope is that they 'see' it finished from Heaven's dimension.

A special man whom I respect and admire is my big brother, Dex Crotts. Over the years, we have crossed many milestones and built thousands of great memories. All my life he, and now my sister-in-law, Ann, have been a reliable source of support, in good times or times of trouble; to offer advice, humor, kindness, and help. I will never be able to find words to express how much they mean to me. Without their help throughout my medical ordeals, I might have lost my business. I love them and I am very proud and grateful to have Dex as my brother.

To my sister-in-law, Angela Hamrick, I would like to express my deepest gratitude for standing by Phyllis through everything, especially the ordeal of my death. When all the attention had to be on me, Angela was the first responder and strong pillar that stood firm and supported my wife. She not only prayed, she was there in person, doing exactly what was needed; speaking up on behalf of her big sister. Just like her name implies, she was an "Angel" who got things done at a time of chaos in our lives! I never had a sister, but I have always loved and claimed Angela as my sister. Phyllis says Angela may be her little sister, but she will always be her hero for much more than can be described here.

To my life-long friend and brother-in-the-Lord, Bishop Duane Swilley, whose encouragement, guidance, support, and patience have made writing this book insightful and fun. I am eternally grateful for his exceptional creative input, and hard work. Without his motivation, expert writing skills, and resolute persistence for me to finish this book, it may have never been completed.

My deepest and sincere appreciation to my Senate Campaign Chairman, Dave Allem and his wife, Sandy. The years of commitment, dedication, and loyalty to me and the campaign, resulted in my election to the Senate. Many details and accomplishments shared in this book would not have been possible without the personal sacrifices made by these two great friends.

My Press Secretary, Wayne Jones, was the first person to respond to me on the ground in front of his store on the fateful day I died. His fast response to administer CPR and calling 911 helped save my life. I cannot thank him and his wife, Mimi, for all their help during this incredible battle of life over death. These two are some of the best friends I've ever known, and I am forever in their debt.

Lieutenant Greg Carson of the Conyers Police Department exemplifies extraordinary dedication to his job and those he serves. When he arrived at the scene, he took over the exhaustive administration of CPR. In addition, he kept a very chaotic atmosphere organized. Then he assisted the ambulance in getting me to the hospital. I have no doubt that this brave man was a vital part of saving my life. As the years pass, I often think of him and will always be grateful to him for going above and beyond the call of duty on that tragic day.

A big thank you to Gail Zapf for her years of dedication as my Senate Administrative Assistant at the Georgia State Capitol. Her college major in journalism, demonstrates her outstanding talent and many hours of expert work she did in editing and proofing this book. Phyllis and I think highly of her and cherish the friendship we have shared for all these years.

A special thanks to Paul, Jan, Matt and Laurie Crouch of Trinity Broadcasting Network (TBN), for their love and friendship, over the past 25 years. I am very grateful to them for opening their ministry to Phyllis and me. Their anointing, along with their most proficient abilities in Christian Broadcasting, have allowed us to share our miracle testimony with millions of people around the world.

TABLE OF CONTENTS

Forward..Page 25

Introduction..Page 27

Chapter 1: Code Blue! Code Blue!............................Page 31

Chapter 2: My Beginnings.......................................Page 35

Chapter 3: The Persuader.......................................Page 41

Chapter 4: O Death, Where is Thy Sting?............ Page 49

Chapter 5: What Now?..Page 63

Chapter 6: Fighting the Good Fight of Faith....... Page 73

Chapter 7: The Power of One..................................Page 81

Chapter 8: Difference in the Gospel & the Gospel

of the Kingdom...Page 87

Chapter 9: Between Heaven and Earth.................Page 93

Chapter 10: Restored ....Page 99

Chapter 11: The Open Door...................................Page 105

Chapter 12: I'm Somewhere in the Future...... Page 111

Meet the Author ....Page 115

FORWARD

It is extremely rare when someone is literally raised from the dead, especially after an extended period of time. This is exactly what happened to Senator Mike Crotts. Even in the Bible, there are only eight other accounts of a person being resurrected from the dead, besides Jesus and those who were resurrected with Him, on the day He defied all human understanding and returned from the grave. God gave Senator Crotts and his wife Phyllis a promise, and Phyllis reminded God of His promise to them in such a powerful and persistent stance of absolute faith, that the miraculous occurred, and that promise was kept.

Years before this event my late husband, Kim Clement, prophesied over this beautiful couple and told them that they would have a son. Kim saw a vital event in their future, a promise of a son, because God knew it would be necessary for them to have this promise to hold up in a tragic and contrary situation that had the potential to destroy their future, and the destiny God had for them. The result of Phyllis remembering and commanding that future into existence was a testimony that few in this world ever have; a testimony that has and will continue to touch lives, bring hope and show the world that God is in control and already knows the trials we will face. God gave us the gift of prophecy, the ability to catch a glimpse of something in our future that will drive us when we reach mountains of resistance and adversity, or even in the face of death. It was because of the hope, that glimpse into what the future held, that Senator Crotts is alive today, and able to share with you his journey back from death and the profound work that God has done in his life since.

Not only is this the most powerful testimony I have seen in my lifetime, but a testimony that bonded Kim and me to this family forever. God brought us together to show His magnificence to a world full of doubt, and for us to form a friendship that lasted for the remainder of Kim's life and one that I will continue to treasure for the remainder of mine.

I know you will be blessed and astounded as you read this incredible story, and I pray that it will speak to you in your own life and encourage you. As Kim always said, "Impossible is nothing for God".

Jane Elizabeth Clement
Co-Founder of *House of Destiny*
Los Angeles, California

INTRODUCTION

Since man's creation, he has marveled at the miracle of birth and agonized over the mystery of death. In birth, one experiences and witnesses a beginning and then an unfolding of various stages of life. In death, one experiences the end of life without knowing exactly what happens afterwards. It is that 'unknown factor' that causes many of us to fear death. One usually cannot experience death and live to tell about it, however having died and returned to life, I want to help in overcoming the anxiety of dying and assure you that there is absolutely no reason to fear death. We simply change dimensions. Like walking from one room into the next.

This book is a firsthand account of how one can experience the impossible, with God's help! *Dead for Thirty-Four Minutes* is a personal out-of-body experience that took me to a heavenly dimension. I actually spoke with God in the form of the Holy Spirit, who revealed not only my purpose on Earth, but what He expects all believers to be doing until Jesus returns. It's not about sitting around, waiting for the rapture or the great escape. We, as the body of Christ, have a work to do until He comes: making *"... the kingdoms of this world, become the Kingdoms of our Lord and of His Christ ..."* Revelation 11:15 (KJV). God explained how our destinies are mastered through a "revelation of John's Revelation." So, as you read this testimony, it is not meant to judge, but to encourage you to embrace life with everything in you, regardless of how much time you have left or whatever circumstances you face.

A heart attack is one way to acquire firsthand knowledge about death. I actually came out of my mortal, corruptible body and experienced my immortal, incorruptible form. This testimony is to help encourage those who do not believe or know God. The fact that there is, indeed, life after death proves to me that He does exist and that the Bible is His inspired Word.

In the book of Ecclesiastes, chapter 3, verses 1 through 8, it tells us that: *(v 1) "There is a time for everything and a season for every activity under heaven"* .... *(v 2) "There is a time to be born and a time to die"* ... *(v 4)" A time to weep and a time to laugh; a time to mourn and a time to dance"* (NKJ).

When we lose a loved one, we feel a void in our heart that causes us to mourn or to grieve, even yearn for that person to be back in our presence. Throughout the grieving process, so many questions run through our minds: Is there really life after death? Is there a heaven? Is there a Hell? Did my loved one suffer during death? Do they still know I'm here? Will I ever see them again?

With the acceptance of Jesus Christ as Lord and Savior, death of our earthly body simply means that we are promised a new body and eternal life with Him; 2 Cor.5:8, (KJV). Many people believe that God does not reveal Himself to man today as He did before the birth of Christ, or while He was here on Earth. Let me assure you, through the Holy Spirit, God is revealing Himself to us as never before. As you read these pages, I hope that my experience of life after death will help you; 1) discover your true destiny and purpose on Earth, 2) help you through the grieving process, 3) ultimately help you overcome the fear of death and, 4) encourage you to rejoice, knowing that your loved ones are totally healed and in the presence of God.

Do not give in to the fear of death; accept it as part of life or a stepping stone into life eternal. Unless, the enemy (devil) tries to take you before your appointed time; *"...it is appointed unto man once to die, but after this the judgment."* Hebrews 9:27 (KJV). then you fight to live with all your might!

Mike D. Crotts
Former Georgia State Senator

Chapter 1

Code Blue! Code Blue!

This chapter is dedicated to the heroic men and women who responded to the emergency call, "person down" that fall afternoon of October 9, 1990, and gave their all in every way, in an effort to save my life.

"Code Blue!" These are the words that medical teams do not like to hear. But, when they do, their full medical attention, knowledge, and experience is immediately implemented to save a life. Words cannot express my heartfelt gratitude to each of the following individuals and organizations for their life saving efforts that day.

Upon their arrival at the scene, paramedics performed CPR, administered IV fluids, and applied emergency defibrillation techniques to restore the normal rhythm of my heart. They shocked me eight or nine times, but my lifeless body did not respond. At anytime, during their efforts they could have said, "He's gone." They could have pronounced me dead, recorded the time, and covered me up, knowing they had done their best to save me. Although I was unresponsive, they refused to give up. Their dedication, tenacity and perseverance deserve the highest commendation and appreciation.

You may wonder why all these people deserve credit for saving my life, when my testimony is about my wife calling me back from death itself. My answer is simple: all the people mentioned here were used by God to save me. I believe everything that was done and every person that participated in life-saving efforts and prayers were ordained by God that day! Until the final call by the emergency room doctors that spoke the final word to my wife that I was dead, and they were just keeping my organs alive, because I was a registered 'organ donor;' that my wife heard the voice of God to call my spirit back into my body. Of course, God gets all the glory, but many obeyed Him and were instrumental in saving my life. These are the special people who were involved that day:

Wayne Jones, Campaign Press Secretary, first responder, administered CPR.

Lieutenant Greg Carson, City of Conyers Police Department / Responding Police Officer, administered CPR, and provided Police escort for the Ambulance en-route to the Hospital.

The Paramedics of National Emergency Medical Services responded and administered medical attention, and transport to the hospital.

The Rockdale County Sheriff's Department and The City of Conyers Police Department blocked all intersections along the entire route to the Hospital for the Police escort and Ambulance.

The Emergency room doctors and nurses at Rockdale County Hospital, now Piedmont Rockdale Medical Center.

Emory University Hospital Doctors, Nurses, staff, and Dr. Paul Walter, Cardiologist.

On my web page, you can watch the video provided by the City of Conyers Police Department. It is the actual police footage that was recorded on the responding police officer's dash cam in his patrol car. The video and audio are not the best quality. When viewing the video, if you turn up the volume, it will help you hear and experience the comments and activity during the time I was on the ground and en-route to the hospital. As you watch the video the elapsed time and date is displayed at the bottom right side of the video.

View the police video at www.mikecrotts.com

Chapter 2

My Beginnings

The first serious recollection about God that I can remember was as a young boy lying in the fresh cut grass, on a warm summer night, staring up at the stars and wondering who made them and how did they get there? As a teenager, these thoughts lingered with me, but like most teens, even though I attended the local Christian (denominational) Church, I was not really 'tuned-in' to deep spiritual revelations. It was, however settled in my mind that God did exist, and He created the Universe; I had accepted Jesus as my Savior, but my interests were nowhere near "serving Him."

In my early twenties, I met and married my wife, Phyllis, whose family members were dedicated church-goers. From the age of five, she was well versed in the Bible. She had so much more than just a knowledge of Him (like I did); she actually had a 'relationship' with God, and she insisted that we pray together every day as a married couple. Phyllis would tell stories of the miracles that her grandmother and great-grandmother witnessed in their lives and I was amazed. One in particular stands out in my mind: Her grandmother was outside watching one of her brothers chop wood when the axe head flung from its handle and the blade ricocheted and hit him in the forehead! Immediately the blood started gushing out and Phyllis' grandmother ran in the house to get her mother. Phyllis' great-grandmother came out, walked up to her son, and placed her hand on the boy's head and said, "Praise the Lord! Praise the Lord!" Then she turned around and walked back into the house, leaving Phyllis' grandmother staring at her brother's fore head and watching it heal back together before her very eyes! I thought (and was taught) that healings and miracles ended when Jesus and all His disciples died. Boy, did I have a lot to learn! However, this was Phyllis' heritage!

The first major disagreement in our marriage stemmed from the vast differences between us concerning God and the church. Who would have thought that two believers or born again Christians would be so different in how they worshipped God? When we dated, our discussions seemed to be more in sync regarding our beliefs than actually seeing it up close and personal as man and wife on a daily basis. Phyllis was a charter-member of a very charismatic, inter-denominational church founded by the pastor, who was the only pastor she had ever known. I, on the other hand, was a member of a fairly large, local Christian-denominational church that had offered a great youth program at the time I joined; and all my teen friends attended mostly for the social aspects. I visited church with Phyllis from time to time, but it wasn't long before the practices and teachings at her church were way too much for me to understand or accept. I found myself mocking and debating with her about the prayers for miracles and I made fun of all the testimonies on Wednesday night services from the members that wanted to praise God for blessing them. I was taught that the teachings about the Holy Spirit, speaking in tongues, and the nine gifts of the Spirit mentioned in the Book of Acts no longer existed. In addition, members of her congregation actually lifted their hands to praise, when singing; the choir rocked out, and they had spiritual dancers that also praised with them! This was so uncomfortable for me because I was used to solemn assemblies and traditional hymns with no outward expressions at all. I decided that we needed to go back to my church and even demanded that she change over to my denomination.

I also made fun of televangelists, including healing and miracle ministries. I believed they planted people in their congregations to deceive others in order to trick them into giving money. Phyllis maintained that my church was like attending a PTA meeting. "No anointing and no Spirit or presence of God there at all" she would say. Our disagreements escalated to the point that each Sunday, we would dress and go our separate ways to our own different churches. This was the only argument or division that we experienced in our marriage, and Phyllis knew that this was not pleasing to the Lord. So, she prayed and asked God to forgive us and give her a plan that would unite us in a church together and ... Man! Did He give her a plan! It was like a stealth bomber that I never saw coming, and it changed my life forever. Being totally unaware of Phyllis' plan from God, she approached me one evening and said, "I know that the Lord is not happy with us arguing and attending different churches on Sunday mornings, so I want to make a deal with you: If you will attend every service with me at my church for one month (Sunday mornings, Sunday nights, and Wednesday nights), then if you still cannot feel comfortable there, I promise to renounce my membership and join your church." Wow! I thought this would be a piece of cake! It was just what I had been waiting for; what a deal! So, I quickly agreed to do it and for the next four weeks, I happily attended her church. After all, I only had to endure this for one month and then I would get my way.

On the last Sunday morning of the month, while driving to church, I quipped with a little bit of sarcasm, "Well, Phyllis are you ready to join my church?" She never said a word, but in her quiet way, with total trust in knowing that she had heard from God, she just smiled and maintained her composure. We sat on the end of the pew with her parents, who slid over to make room. During the service, I really could not tell you what the pastor preached that Sunday morning, I'm sure it was a good sermon, because he was a dynamic preacher, but my wife leaned over to her right and whispered to her mother something like, "Where do you guys want to go eat after church?" As the service was coming to a conclusion, before the Pastor opened the alter for prayer as was the custom, it was like I had been 'translated' from my seat to the pulpit, finding myself standing next to the pastor, weeping and saying, "I want to join this church!" My first experience of a small (?) miracle, with many more to come. That was in 1972 and I remained a member, a deacon, and a church leader there until the death of our pastor in 2009.

Thinking back now on that miraculous event and how I have grown spiritually, I am so grateful to God for leading me in the right direction and for giving me the wisdom to ask this woman of faith to be my wife. By-the-way, you might also like to know that I got to apologize to a couple of those healing Evangelists from TV that I had mocked, (i.e., Oral Roberts & Benny Hinn) and asked them to forgive me for judging their ministries. Needless to say, it has definitely been a learning process for me. I was blessed with great teachers and spiritual leaders who explained the Bible in ways that made me understand as a child learns in a school classroom. I was making big adjustments in my spiritual walk and I began to develop a new hunger for more of this great book called the Bible. I felt God's presence for the first time and learned how to pray more effectively; and how tithing really works. I learned not only about Jesus and what He did and expects from us, but met and received the Third Person in the Trinity, called the Holy Spirit. He is much more than what I had ever known, my comprehension included how He fits in the *now* of things.

My yielding to Him increased my faith, strengthened my marriage, increased my personal relationships, and made me more successful in my business. But most importantly, now I could hear from God for myself. People around me were seeing a difference in my attitude and actions, but I still had a lot to learn. Making a life, as a man, entails a lot of pressure in general. However, my pressures were nowhere near the pressures my father suffered. This is who raised me and taught me the most about life.

Chapter 3

The Persuader

One of the biggest things I see in new converts is their zeal. They are so inspired by their new revelation of God that they want to get everyone saved. This is a normal reaction after salvation. Unfortunately, sometimes their eagerness becomes aggressive and ends up turning off a lot of people. We have to remember everything is in God's timing. His desire is that we will ask Him into our hearts. He gives us that choice and it is not for you or me to decide when that will happen in another person's life. We can share the good news and leave the rest to God. I'll give you an example of what I did that partially postponed my Fathers salvation.

After my spiritual experiences, every time I saw my Dad, I would make sure I talked to him about accepting Jesus. I was relentless; "Don't you want to live forever? Don't you want to see your Mother again?" I was so eager that I was totally blind to the fact that I was pushing him farther away from salvation. He would simply say, "When you're dead, you're dead. There's no life after that! Mike, I believe in freedom 'of" religion and 'from' religion."

My Dad was a proud humanitarian. He was a unique man whose character and integrity easily out-shone many Christians. Unknowingly, he lived biblical principles his whole life. So why did he feel the way he did? During the economic depression of the 1930's, my Dad, his sister, and his mother walked, slept beside the road covered with newspaper to stay warm, and hitched rides, from North Carolina to Atlanta, Georgia to find work. He sold newspapers to make what little money he could to help the three of them. With a third grade education he went on to become a very successful businessman, a self made man. Although he was blindly practicing Christian principles, God blessed him in spite of his unbelief (Matt. 5:45). Even though he didn't believe in God, he attended church with my mother, my brother Dex, and me. He worked in the community, constantly gave to others, instilled good moral values and guidance in my brother and me so that we would grow up to live successful lives. Along life's path he had several bad experiences with unethical ministers. Their shady actions caused him to unjustly judge all pastors as self preservationists. This moved him farther away from God, and there I was continually badgering him to accept Jesus and go to church.

Even my mother could see it and would tell me to just give him some time. Moms have a loving way of saying, "back off, son!" In spite of my pushing, my father's love for me helped him understand that my concern was for him. The last time I said something to him about being saved, he said, "Son, I believe all your spiritual experiences are real to you, but I still believe when you're dead, you're dead." About a month later, he told Phyllis that he didn't want to hurt me, but really wished that I would not talk to him about it anymore. Phyllis told him that she would talk to me about it and get me to stop. Her spiritual wisdom and understanding is extremely accurate and precise, but it is also patient and gentle. Knowing that he was turned off she said, "I assure you that it will not happen again if you will make me a promise. I know that you do not believe God is real but I'm going to pray that God will reveal Himself to you. And when He does, promise me that you will accept Him!" My dad thought a long minute and replied with a smile, "Okay, If He ever reveals Himself to me, I promise to accept Him." When he made that promise to her, she knew he would keep his word. Phyllis came to me and explained what he had said and the promise he had made to her and from that day, I never mentioned it to him again.

In 2002, my mother had a kidney procedure in the hospital that caused an allergic reaction from the contrast dye that was injected into her veins for x-rays. Her blood pressure and oxygenation level dropped drastically, and the doctors told my dad that if they continued to fall, she would not live through the night. My dad immediately called Dex and me to come to the hospital. My brother lived farthest away, so Phyllis and I arrived first. Mother's condition had not improved. Weeping, my dad turned to us and said, "I need you to call on your 'religion' to help her, please." He loved her so much. They had been married for sixty-six years and he was desperate.

To my surprise Phyllis spoke up and said, "No! *You* have authority over her and *you're* the head of your household. *You* need to pray for her and we will agree with you!" I was shocked! Did I just hear my wife say that we would not pray? In that moment when he asked for prayer, the Spirit of the Lord spoke to Phyllis and said, "Speak to him about authority." Phyllis knew that he was a man of authority and that he understood that word. I pulled her off to the side and asked, "Why in the world would you tell him that you would not pray for my mother? I can't believe you would do that." She reminded me, "I didn't say I would not pray." She then told me how she had only yielded to God and spoke exactly what He had told her to say. In other words, He was speaking to my Dad through Phyllis.

Later that evening, Dad went home, crawled into bed and, in the stillness of the night, he slipped out of bed, knelt down to pray and made a deal with the Lord. He told me that he said something like, "God, if you are real, please heal my wife and allow me to die first. I will accept You in my heart, get baptized, go to church every week, and serve you the rest of my days left on earth." During the night my mother's condition improved so much that she was sitting up talking to everyone the next morning. Dad, Phyllis, my brother Dex, his wife Ann were there in her room telling her how she almost died. My Dad closed the door and announced that he had something to say. He looked at my mother and told her that he had prayed for her the night before and made a promise to God. Ann gently said, "Thurmon, we all prayed for her." Immediately Dad turned and pointed his long finger upward saying, "Yes, but I had authority!" Phyllis was so excited! She knew by this statement that he had received the Word of the Lord. He continued to explain how he had gone home and prayed and surrendered to God, who told him he had the authority to speak life to her and my Mother was totally healed. God had really revealed Himself to my Dad! From that day forward, he kept his word to God. He was saved at eighty-two, baptized at eighty-three, and attended church (even if it was the little Chapel at the Independent Living facility) every Sunday until he died at age eighty-seven. What a miracle! I am so grateful to God and for a wife who hears from the Lord. All of my pressing and pushing him was to no avail but one word from God, "Authority," reserved my dad's eternal place in Heaven. I learned a great lesson from this experience, I know that God is aware of all our circumstances and we need to pray by the Spirit, stay out of His way, and see His mercy and grace.

Most of the time people get so busy and concerned about what they need and want in life, that they lose sight of their true Source; God. Sometimes we become so engrossed in ourselves and our own selfish desires that we start doing things our own way, which can cause unnecessary stress that ultimately affects our health. Anyone, including Christians, can do this and not even realize it. This is exactly what I was doing even though I thought I was serving the Lord. I was on life's treadmill, thinking things were going well and that I was actually yielding to God's will. However, there were still many things I had not surrendered to Him. Important things. For example, on one hand, I was praying for God's help and purpose for my life, yet on the other hand, I would take it out of God's hands and do it my own way. Little did I know that I was about to experience my first encounter with my own personal healing.

On September 15, 1973, after having lunch with my Dad and brother, we returned to our office and I suddenly noticed a pain in my side. It felt so excruciating that I decided to go home and lie down. As the afternoon wore on, the pain intensified, and I felt nauseous and deathly sick. Phyllis insisted I go to the emergency room, but being the macho man, I told her I could take it and would be fine. She was not satisfied with that, so she called my Dad, "the Persuader," who came to the rescue and simply said with authority that I could let him take me to the hospital or an ambulance would be called. I knew he meant what he said so I got in his car with Phyllis by my side and went to the emergency room.

After going through all the medical tests, it was determined that I had kidney stones. There's no way I can understand the pain level for natural childbirth, but the medical personnel in the ER said the pain for kidney stones is equal to, or worse than giving birth. From that day forward, I felt a new compassion for all mothers! After a few days in the hospital, the kidney stones passed, and I was sent home, only to return two days later with double pneumonia. This was caused by a staph infection contracted while being treated for the kidney stones. As a result of being bedridden for more than a week, hooked up to IVs and oxygen, a blood clot developed in my leg, passed through my heart, causing a mild coronary infarction. The clot then traveled to my left lung, causing pulmonary embolism. In laymen's terms. pulmonary embolism occurs when a blood clot gets wedged in the artery and deprives the lung of oxygen. I was a very sick man, on the brink of death. By the time my heart rate returned to normal; the clot had destroyed most of the lower lobe of my left lung. My church pastor, the congregation, and all of my family members prayed for me and the Lord healed me. This was my first experience with a personal miracle and the healing power of God. To this day my chest x-rays show nothing more than faint scar tissue in that lower lobe of my lung where the blood clot had lodged. Not that long ago, I had made fun of healing, miracles, and God's ability to use doctors for His purposes. Yet I was raised up for another day and given exactly what I had denied.

We can never anticipate how God will use the circumstances in our lives to help us, so that we become a living testimony to His glory. When we face adversity, God always uses it to perfect us. Many people have a difficult time understanding this truth because of their inability to see beyond natural circumstances. We limit God with our minds of reason and lack of faith. I believe that is why so many people ask, "Why did God do this to me? Why did He let this happen? God must be punishing me for something I did wrong." No, God does not cause these things, nor does He do things to punish us. He is a loving heavenly Father who only wants the best for us always. As earthly parents, do we want the best for our children? Of course, we do. We give them advice and direction and hope they make the right decisions and choices, but if not, we still love them and try to help them through life. Our heavenly Father also gives us the ability to make choices just like He did with Adam and Eve in the Garden of Eden. Sometimes we make choices that allow the enemy to cause us heartaches and sorrows. Yet, in spite of making bad decisions, God still loves us and wants us to learn from our mistakes. Genesis 50:20, says, *"But as for you, you meant evil against me; but God meant it for good, in order to bring it about as it is this day, to save many people alive" (NKJ).*

As I reflect on that tumultuous period in my life, I was guilty of asking God why He allowed me to get sick. It was not God that made me sick; it was the enemy who wanted to kill me; It is written: *"Be self-controlled and alert. Your enemy, the devil, prowls around like a roaring lion looking for someone to devour"* 1 Peter 5:8, (NIV).

Chapter 4

Oh Death, Where is thy Sting?

For sixteen years after joining Phyllis' church, I continued to serve the Lord. I became a Deacon in the church and joined her in teaching two hundred and fifty children, ages six to twelve in our Sunday night children's church service. Teaching this class was very rewarding because we did not have children of our own but wanted them very much. I also continued to operate my real estate and insurance business and participated in community events through our local Kiwanis Club. In late October of 1986, a group of friends in my local Kiwanis Club approached me and asked if I would consider running for the Georgia State Senate.

Politics and governing had never been of any particular interest to me, aside from their possible affects to my real estate business. Rezoning properties through local governments from time to time and assisting local government in rewriting zoning codes was the extent of my expertise. Of course, I was flattered by the suggestion of running for public office, but I gracefully declined and offered to help find someone who would run for our district's Senate seat. Life was good, but the requests for me to run for state senator would not go away.

After an exhaustive but unsuccessful search for potential candidates and the continual encouragement from my friends, I finally agreed to run for our district's State Senate seat for the 1989-90 term. I challenged one of the most powerful senators in the Capitol who served as the Governor's floor leader and Chairman of the Senate Appropriations Committee. It was a tough campaign, and I lost after earning 46% of the vote, which was not bad for a first time run. I was not about to give up. I had learned a lot from that first campaign, but it could never prepare me for what I was about to face in the next race two years later. In December of 1989, our son Caleb was born, and Phyllis and I were immersed in our new role as the happy, proud parents we always wanted to be.

In May of 1990, I filed the paperwork and qualified to run for the same senate seat, against the same incumbent for the 1991-92 term of the Georgia General Assembly. Three weeks prior to the election on a beautiful fall day, I met my wife, our 10-month old son, and Phyllis' grandmother for lunch. My calendar was full that day: I was scheduled to debate my opponent that afternoon, then go back to the campaign office and meet with Wayne Jones, my press secretary, to work on the final campaign ads we would be using before election day. The debate went well. I headed back to the campaign office, called Wayne to give him an update, and he said he was finishing up some work at his shop and would join me soon. It had been a good day. The weather was perfect, and I figured since Wayne's shop was in the same shopping center as the campaign headquarters, I'd just walk over to his place. I was just outside his door and I suddenly felt so dizzy that I blacked out. We learned later from the attending physician that I had experienced a complete heart block and was dead before I even hit the ground.

Wayne Jones' wife, Mimi, witnessed my collapse from their storefront window and shouted to Wayne to call 911. He ran out to me and began administering CPR, using only the breathing portion of the procedure. He was so upset and concerned for me that he forgot to do the chest compressions. A short time later, police officer Greg Carson, responded to the call and arrived before the paramedics. He pulled up to the scene with a camcorder on the dashboard of his patrol car that began recording the entire event from the time he received the call, with the date and time flashing on the video. He also wore a microphone on his shoulder that recorded the audio portion. Officer Carson took over administering CPR, including the chest compressions until the paramedics arrived. When they arrived, they continued to perform CPR and also used defibrillator paddles to shock my heart many times. Throughout this process, the time and date are flashing on the dash-cam video and the paramedics' comments are audible. saying, "We've had no pulse for five minutes," "No pulse for ten minutes," "No pulse for fifteen minutes." Eventually, you hear them say, "He's gone. He's dead." These professionals could have called it quits, pronounced me dead, covered me up and went on their way, but they would not give up! They continued CPR and shocked me numerous times while lying on the ground, and also in the ambulance. By now, we were en-route to our local hospital, with the Conyers Police Department going out of their way to block the heavy five o'clock traffic for the ambulance to go as fast as they could.

As my lifeless body was laying on the sidewalk, my spirit had crossed over into another dimension. I was clinically dead in my flesh, but alive in the spirit. Surprisingly, this death transition was as easy as walking through a door from one room to another, with no pain whatsoever. I can totally relate to the scripture, *"O death, where is thy sting? O grave, where is thy victory?"* 1Cor. 15:55 (KJV). I suddenly found myself in the most beautiful, magnificent *garden* with indescribable colors and clarity. The waters flowed in rippling brooks through the adjoining gardens and were crystal clear; the colors of the flowers, grass, trees, and the blue skies were more vivid like none I have ever seen. This place was breathtaking! On the horizon, were hills and mountains that radiated with an almost blinding light behind them, like a sunrise, I could feel it drawing me there. As I floated through the meadow toward the garden, the Holy Spirit joined me. Our communication was spirit to spirit, just like I hear from Him in my prayers. I noticed my spiritual body was quite a bit younger looking. "What is this all about?" I asked. The Holy Spirit then took me to a magnificent grassy knoll that was covered with a blanket of gorgeous colorful flowers that overlooked a rippling brook. The aroma was exquisite, and the sounds were so relaxing and peaceful.

With His voice He commanded the flowing waters to become very still. Images, one after the other, appeared on the surface of the water like a movie screen. I saw each world system labeled like Caleb's mountain in *Joshua 14:12-14* designated to be conquered; Government, Learning, Outreach, Business, Entertainment, Family, and Media. "What does this mean?" I asked. The Spirit of the Lord said, "These are My kingdoms or world systems. They are kingdoms that the enemy (devil) has taken from my people. These systems are failing, and it is time for My church universal, my people, to take these kingdoms back. I have given everyone a purpose. No matter how small or insignificant they may think, their purpose is part of my plan to bring My Kingdom back to earth." Then, I remembered studying these scriptures, *"Then the seventh angel sounded: And there were loud voices in heaven, saying, "The kingdoms of this world have become the Kingdoms of our Lord and of His Christ, and He shall reign forever and ever!"* (Revelation 11:15, NKJ). Another scripture came to me so clearly, *"Now if you obey me fully and keep my covenant, then out of all nations you will be my treasured possession. Although the whole earth is mine, you will be for me a kingdom of priests and a holy nation"* Ex 19: 5-6, (NIV).

When the world systems fail, the non-believers of the world will turn to the Church for solutions. God said to me, "This is why it is necessary for the Church to be prepared and educated in all these systems of the world, so they can give the world the solutions and show them how to take back the kingdom I have placed them in, as I intended it to be from the beginning." I also remembered another scripture regarding this saying, *"The whole earth groans; waiting for the manifestation of the sons of God."* Ro. 8:19-22 (KJV).

He then told me that I was going back to the earthly dimension to be involved in government or the political arena to make a difference. I realized at that point that 'we' have a work to do. We cannot just sit here on earth and wait for the "great escape!" At that moment I knew how Moses felt when he said, *"Don't send me; send someone else, like my brother"* (Exodus 4:10-14). I whispered to the Lord that I really did not want to go back to earth; I wanted to go over there, pointing to the bright horizon that I believe, on the other side, was Heaven. "No, you are going back to earth, said the Lord." I pleaded with Him just to let me stay in this beautiful garden, "I will be happy to spend eternity here." The Lord said, "You will take the 'Garden mentality' back with you as well as the 'Kingdom principles.' You will carry this knowledge and My presence with you the rest of your life. People will be drawn to you because of this experience and they will want what you have; which is simply 'more of Me.' You will not preach, I have many assigned to communicate this revelation, but you will demonstrate these principles and show there is more of Me than the salvation experience, the baptism in water experience, the baptism of the Holy Spirit experience, and the experience of deliverance from evil spirits. You will share with them the experience of the Rule of Christ and how to make Jesus, the King and Lord of your life!"

Although I was fully aware of my wife and son back on Earth, I still pleaded with God to let me stay. I even begged Him to bring my wife and son to me. Once again, He said, "You are going back." He began to flood my mind with spiritual knowledge and fresh new interpretations of the Bible. The very last thing I remember Him saying to me: "When you return, there will be things you experienced here that you will remember immediately, but there will be some things that you will only remember as I reveal then to you again in the fullness of time."

This illustrates the scripture *"Faith without works is dead."* (James 2:26, KJV). To some this scripture might seem like a contradiction, but we are justified by grace through faith, and the natural result of faith in the heart is 'works' that all can see. We have received Jesus by faith and His righteousness before God; these things flow from a regenerated heart (Titus 3:5) & (1 Cor. 6:9-10). When we have been regenerated by the Holy Spirit, our lives will demonstrate that new life. Our works will be characterized by obedience to God.

Then in Matthew 7:16-23, it says, *"By their fruits you will know them"* ... *"Not everyone who says to Me, 'Lord, Lord', will enter the Kingdom of Heaven, but only the one who does the will of My Father in Heaven. Many will say to Me in that day, 'Lord, Lord, did we not prophesy in your name? Did we not drive out demons in your name? Did we not do mighty deeds in your name? Then I will declare to them solemnly, "I never knew you! Depart from Me, you workers of iniquity!"* "Knowing" Him requires intimacy. In Gen 4:1, it speaks of Adam 'knowing' his wife and she conceived a child. God wants the closest union or relationship possible with us. Of course, I am speaking of a 'spiritual' intimacy, not the flesh.

As the Spirit of the Lord was telling me all this, Phyllis was in the emergency room taking in everything that was happening and waiting for our pastor to arrive to pray for me. No one came at that time, so she asked if she could be allowed in the room to see me and pray. They told her that I had been without oxygen too long and that they were just keeping my organs alive because my drivers' license showed that I was an organ donor. They asked her to wait in a room where the hospital chaplain would come and talk to her. When she refused, a couple of hospital staff took her by the arms and assisted her in the direction away from the ER room. In the process, she jerked her arms loose and hit her right hand on a steel doorframe. Phyllis' sister, Angela arrived shortly thereafter and assessed the situation and was very adamant about getting Phyllis in to see me, to the point that the hospital administrator was called. After seeing the huge hematoma on the back of Phyllis' hand, the administrator agreed to allow my wife in to see me. Here, in Phyllis' own words, is the rest of the story:

PHYLLIS: When I entered the room, I noticed that Mike was lying flat on his back, naked, with his head arched back. A nurse was sitting on a stool at his head, giving him oxygen through a large bulb-like instrument, which went down his throat and that she manually had to keep mashing. His clothes had been cut off and they were hanging down from the gurney. His legs were placed in pull-out rests, spread eagle, facing the door. His face was ashen-white, and his lips were royal purple. He had round, blackish-brown burn marks all over his chest and his stomach was very swollen, as though he was nine months pregnant. I asked why he was so swollen and was told that he was accidentally given oxygen through his esophagus rather than his trachea, so his stomach was full of oxygen. He was hooked up to several mechanical devices/machines and they still had IVs running.

Everyone in the room was wearing a mask. One of the medical attendants turned to me and said gently, "Mrs. Crotts, we need to get him downstairs to the morgue to harvest his organs." My heart sank, and all I could remember were the words from a prophet named Kim Clement. We had visited a conference the previous year, where he was the speaker, and called Mike out to say, "You are anointed to do a work in politics in the Kingdom of God and to lead your son in the same direction." Well, he had not done this yet and our son was only ten months old. No pastor had arrived yet to pray, so I knew in my heart that it was not Mike's time to die and that I must try to pray. A voice inside me said, "Do it now! Call him back!"

Trembling, I stepped forward and grabbed both his ankles, and with a loud voice I called out his name saying, "Michael!!! Get back in your body, in the name of Jesus!!!" You could have heard a pin drop. Then, the heart monitor started beeping. Even though I could only see the attendant's eyes because of their masks, I could tell they were all surprised. I was immediately whisked out and they started working on Mike again. After about an hour, one of the ER doctors came out and told me that Mike was 'technically alive' but that he was probably brain dead. After all, he had been without oxygen for over 34 minutes. Weeping, I thanked the doctor and told him and the ER team, that I appreciated them and was aware of their medical knowledge and that each one had given their very best, but none of them had the last word over my husband. By then, one of our associate pastors, Sam Lalaian had arrived, and was allowed to go in and see Mike for a couple of minutes, who was much more 'composed' than me. However, he did not have a clue what I had just done, but I knew Pastor Sam was in agreement for a miracle.

Even though I spoke what was in my heart, my thoughts could not help wondering if I had done the wrong thing. Brain dead?! To be dead while you yet live is not what I had in mind when I prayed and called him back. I ran to the restroom and cried out to the Lord asking Him if this was how he would be healed? Neither Mike nor I would want him to live like a vegetable. All of a sudden, I felt a physical manifestation of peace come over me like someone was pouring warm thick honey on my head and down my entire body. When the feeling reached my feet, I was as calm as could be. I also had a reassurance that Mike was going to be fine and from that moment on, I did not waiver in faith or doubt, nor was I afraid again. I told my sister, Angela, that Mike was going to be fine and she agreed with me in faith. The words to a popular song at that time came to my mind that would not leave me; it was titled *"Whose Report Will You Believe?"* Answer in song: *"We shall believe the report of the Lord!"*

The waiting room was full of people, reporters from the local newspaper, and a photographer. The nurses felt sorry for me and allowed me to use their restroom facility, so I didn't have to endure all the questions or have my photo taken. By then, I was already hearing the stories from several people mixing up the truth of what had happened to Mike. A very nice lady, Peggy Fry and her son, Chad, were in the emergency room next to us, getting his broken arm set and they heard everything, especially me calling Mike back! She said, "It made the hairs on my arms and neck stand straight up!" She gave me her phone number and said that if I ever needed someone to confirm what happened that day, she would be happy to help. I didn't understand at the time, but later when many 'forgot' the events as they really happened, I was so grateful I had her to vouch for us.

When a brain-wave test was done from his room in the CICU, the prognosis was that Mike did have some brain activity, but he was severely brain damaged. Again, I thanked the doctor and smiled with my 'peace' intact. Dr. Rose decided to transfer him to another hospital for more intensive tests and treatment. Although Mike was in a coma, he was placed in a drug-induced state of paralysis as well. Due to the oxygen deprivation, he was having muscle spasms so intense, that they caused the IVs and life-support tubes to come out. The paralysis made the doctor concerned that if he woke up from the coma, he might be frightened because he could not move anything from his neck down. Doctor Rose also mentioned the likelihood, at the very best, that Mike would have a ten to fifteen year memory loss. He suggested that I prepare some questions to ask Mike, when he regained consciousness, in order to find out how far back his memory loss and brain damage might be. As I sat there thinking of things to ask, it occurred to me that fifteen years ago was when he joined my church, received the Holy Spirit, and started to grow spiritually. I suddenly realized that if the devil couldn't kill him physically, he would try spiritually. Plus, I would look fifteen years older and he would not even remember our ten month old son. This was heartbreaking, but I still felt that peace of God and remained calm, hoping and praying he would soon wake up.

That night, I had my questions ready, sitting in a straight chair watching and about to sip a cup of water, when I looked and saw Mike's eyes open and stare straight ahead. I jumped out of the chair, dropped my water, and stood beside his bed. As he looked my way, he started trying to speak with a tube down one nostril and a bigger one in his mouth. It took a few times, but I finally made out his words, "Where is Caleb?" I started jumping up and down, praising the Lord, tearing up the list I had made, and yelling out to the nurses, "He remembers Caleb!" They rushed into the room and asked, "Who is Caleb?" I said, "He is our 10 month old son ... he remembers our son!" No fifteen year memory loss here!

Mike's brother, Dex arrived around 9:00 PM to see him and was very concerned about the paralysis and doctor's prognosis. He was so happy to see Mike wake up knowing their parents would not have to see him like that. When his parents arrived at midnight from out of town, Mike started telling them about things on his desk at the office, so they could help carry on his business. Proof positive, for us at least, that there was no brain damage, nor any memory loss. We were all ecstatic to say the least. He was still too fragile to be flown in a helicopter, so the next morning, we went the long way, in an ambulance over 30 miles away at a speed of approximately 25 MPH on the expressway. He stayed one more week in ICU and a couple days in a regular room on the cardiac floor at Emory University Hospital in Atlanta, Georgia. His cardiologist, Dr. Paul Walter, said Mike's case was truly unusual.

When Mike was released from Emory hospital, Dr. Walter showed me the file, and I wept as I read the words written on a sticky note on Mike's chart, ***"Healed by the power of God."*** He looked at Mike and said, "I cannot believe that you are standing here. The odds of anyone living through what you experienced is near zero. Even the small percentage who do live have severe brain damage and are typically on a ventilator." Not Mike, he had experienced a real miracle of God and we cannot thank Him or praise Him enough.

(Ends Phyllis' testimony)

Chapter 5

What Now?

Now that things were beginning to get back to normal, I really did not understand or comprehend all that had been revealed to me. The only thing I could do is take each day waiting on the Lord to show me the things that I needed to do. One of the most difficult things for me was waiting and not knowing how I would begin my purpose and destiny. As I said, patience is not one of my virtues. All I knew was that I was to get involved in politics and make a difference. I remember when I woke up in the hospital and things had settled down after my miraculous return, Phyllis said, "What are you going to do about your campaign?" My response was, "Are you kidding me? I am going to continue my campaign! After what the Lord has shown me that I am to do, there is no way I will lose this race." Well, I did lose, but not by much. I garnered 49.6% of the vote, practically from my hospital bed!

As days and months passed, I began to take issue with the Lord, "You raised me from the dead, told me to get involved in politics, and I have publicly talked about your revelation for my life. Now you let me lose and caused me embarrassment among my peers!" I was really struggling with trying to understand why the Lord seemed to have abandoned me when He was the one who told me to get involved. Did I miss something? Wasn't I supposed to run for the Senate? I even began to question if my out-of-body experience was real. Even after all the miracles, I started feeling sorry for myself and had a pity-party. I simply could not understand why this had happened, and I continued to question the Lord about why he did not let me win. After several months, with no concrete answers, I began to take a look at myself. Could there be something I did that caused me to lose the election?

Sometimes when things do not go our way, we tend to think that everyone and everything is against us, including God. As I reflected on this, I remembered the Bible saying our *'mind is the battleground,'* II Cor. 10:3-5 (KJV). If we allow the enemy to infiltrate our minds with negative thoughts and we accept those thoughts as being normal, then we open ourselves up for the negative (and even death) to enter into our soul. I certainly did not want that to happen, so I asked the Lord why I had lost the race. The difference was that now I was 'asking" Him instead of 'blaming' Him.

Evidently, this was exactly what He had been waiting to hear. Even though I could not see it at the time, " I " was the reason I had lost the race. The Lord revealed to me, in prayer, that the reason I lost was because of my own ego. He made it clear that I had been sent back to make a difference in the political arena, and if I had won that race, my attitude would have been all about 'me' and not the glory of God. I would have been too wrapped up in myself, thinking and saying, "Look what I did!" instead of being humble and recognizing what He planned to do through me. The truth hurts sometimes, but that was exactly what I was doing. I was blaming everyone and everything around me for my misfortunes. When, in fact, I was the problem. When I finally understood, I ask the Lord to forgive me for ever questioning Him. Once my sense of direction was corrected, I began to pray and believe that my purpose and destiny really was in politics and things began to change. I could now see that, if I had won that race, I would have hindered God's will for my whole life. Never forget that God knows all about your past, your present, *and* your future. In my case, losing the first two races didn't matter to God; He knew my future included winning the third race and I would serve the following twelve years unopposed.

My third run for the 1993-94 senate term was not without problems. I had a new opponent and reapportionment had changed the senate district. This meant having to learn new district counties and new constituent issues and concerns. The challenge became more difficult because the shortness of time until the election. Finding new volunteers, staff members, building relationships with the local officials within the new district; at the same time, personally campaigning to get out the votes. The present senator of this particular district was going to Washington to run for Congress leaving the senate seat vacant. He helped introduce me to a lot of local people willing to help. We worked very hard and put in long hours to get the job done. We overcame many obstacles, but I felt this was definitely 'my' time to win. Even the pressures came out positive. I knew from the past two races, how to pace myself for this one. On election night, we all were at the courthouse waiting for the votes to come in and when Phyllis and I saw for sure that I had secured the necessary votes, we shouted, "Praise the Lord!" What a great feeling!

Now what? Phyllis and I took a short vacation and then my senate training began in Athens, Georgia where I learned all the legislative procedures, rules, etc. I began my 12 year tenure in the session of January of 1993.

If you do not have a clear understanding or vision of your purpose and destiny, be patient, keep praying, and ask the Lord for His will and direction in your life. He will certainly show you. Contrary to popular belief, God is NOT in control!! If He were, there would be no murders, rapes, child molestation, or cancers/HIV, etc., etc. God limited Himself by giving 'us' a will and a choice in everything. He did not create us to be robots going around, lifting our hands saying, "Praise the Lord!" Not everything revolves around you in the context of the bigger plan. It's about what you can do to make a difference by influencing your own surroundings and people. Kim Clement once told me that "warfare is proof that the enemy (the devil) has discerned your future." Here's a great example:

New warfare began the day I was to be sworn in at the State Capitol. The families of all the new senators-elect were invited to our swearing-in ceremony, so Phyllis and Caleb had to drive about 25 miles in the pouring down rain that day. At one point on the expressway, the rain became so torrential that she could not see one car-length ahead of her. She noticed cars were stopping on the right shoulder to wait out the storm, but she was in the left lane and fearful about crossing two lanes of traffic to pull over. With the median wall to her left, she continued carefully when she heard tires squealing with that sound of someone trying to slam on their brakes! To her right, a car was spinning out of control and heading directly toward her. She braced for the impact crying out, "JESUS! Help me!"

Determined to avoid the median, she concentrated on looking straight ahead when a beautiful 9 ft. tall man in a shimmering garment appeared, holding his outstretched hand toward her. She quickly glanced to her right again and saw a second very tall man in a shiny garment appear and stand with his hand outstretched toward the spinning car. Both men had shoulder length hair (one light and one dark) with beautiful countenances and she could only see their heads and hands, no wings. In that moment, surrounded with peace and wisdom, Phyllis knew to take her foot off the pedal and just coast as the spinning car next to her regained control. Less than a mile down the expressway, the rain stopped, and the sun came out. Phyllis said the devil immediately started trying to sow doubt in her mind and rob her of the miracle she had just experienced. From the security of his safety seat in the back, our 3-year-old son asked, "Mommy, was that Jesus?" With tears in her eyes, she answered, "No, son, I believe they are our guardian angels." For the rest of the way to the Capitol, they both sang praise songs to the Lord.

Consider this: your pulpit and church just might be in the world system, kingdom, or mountain that God has placed you in. If so, take it for Him! You will be perfected during the process. He will let you have it when He can trust you totally. Read the story of Caleb in the Bible. God gave him a mountain to conquer at 85 years old, because Caleb *"wholly followed God all the days of his life!"* (Joshua 14: 6-14). Here's one example of how I tried to influence my surroundings: In the halls of the Capitol and on the floor of the Senate, I never shied away from the fact that I was a Christian. I didn't wear my faith on my sleeve nor did I ever try to force my beliefs on anyone. My purpose was and is to make a difference in the 'Kingdom of Politics' (or Government).

The Bible says, *"Let your light so shine before men that they may see your good works, and glorify your Father which is in heaven."* Matthew 5:16 (NKJ). When I understood my purpose, receiving credit or attention became unimportant because recognition was not my goal (maybe the reason it's taken me so long to write this book). Remember, my goal was and is to influence my surroundings. What I discovered in doing this was that most of the time I received the credit even though that was not my motive.

It takes diplomacy to present your ideas in a way that allows others to see and understand your ideas, while giving them the opportunity to express theirs. When you do this, it puts your opponent at ease; they let their defenses down. When this happens, they often open up because you are showing interest in their ideas as well. I also found that listening to them, sometimes made my idea(s) better; incorporating some of their ideas into mine, they became involved with the results and usually ended up supporting legislation that I wanted to introduce.

Ego is a powerful thing. I watched other Senators who were so wrapped up in getting credit for legislation that they would allow a great idea that would benefit all citizens, to die in a committee rather than allow anyone else to get credit for the bill. I remember when I was in the minority party, I had a number of bills that I would like to introduce, however, I knew there was no way I could get the votes from the other side to pass the bill. So, I would position myself next to a group of Senators in the opposing political party and talk with someone in my political party, telling them what I was going to introduce. I would make sure I said it loud enough for them to 'overhear' and the next thing I knew they were introducing 'my' legislation. *"Behold, I send you forth as sheep in the midst of wolves: be ye therefore wise as serpents, and harmless as doves"* (Matt. 6:16). So, I think you could say that I influenced my surroundings. It was not something that I wanted credit for, it was what was good for the people, and I obeyed the Lord. To God be the Glory. My purpose was to make a difference, not to get personal credit.

Years later, when I became the ranking Senator and Vice-chairman of the Senate Republican caucus in the State of Georgia, there were times when we would leave the senate floor to privately caucus on legislation that was currently being debated. During a caucus, the leadership would make the decision to vote for or against the legislation or offer floor amendments. Sometimes it would be done for the sole purpose to delay or ultimately make the bill so bad that it could not get the votes needed to pass. Other times the vote was not to support the bill. I would ask, "Why not? This is good for our state and the people you represent." They would answer, "Well, we don't want the other side to get credit for this bill." My response was, "Listen, we are not always right on our issues and neither are they, but on this issue, they are right, and this is good legislation for everyone in your districts back home. So, when we go back on the floor I am going to vote with the other side." They would get furious with me and say that I was not a team player. My response was, "I am a team player, I am on the people's team. I was not elected and sent here to play games, I was elected to represent the people."

Unfortunately, that is what is wrong with politics or government today. It is about gaining more power, getting reelected, who is going to get the credit for passing the bill? What can we do to force a vote on legislation that will make the other side look bad, so it can be used against them in the next election cycle? The process has become so partisan that it is almost impossible to get significant legislation passed. What a travesty to the citizens that elect and place their trust in fellow citizens to represent them in the House of Representatives and in the Senate.

Once I began to settle in my position as a Senator and the word began to get around about my spiritual testimony, I wanted to acknowledge the fine men and women that deserve our respect. Police officers and Paramedics rarely receive the recognition and accolades they so richly deserve. These people helped save my life, and I had the honor of presenting them with a 'privileged resolution' on the floor of the senate to acknowledge the life-saving efforts of police lieutenant, Greg Carson, and my press secretary, Wayne Jones. First responders rush to the scene not knowing what they may find, but they're front line emergency and expertise save lives every day. For that, they have my eternal gratitude.

Not long after, word spread about my 'death to life' experience, and Phyllis and I were invited to give our testimony on Trinity Broadcasting Network (TBN). Following our appearance on TBN, we were asked to speak at various conferences and churches here at home and abroad, sharing our testimony and the miracles of God in our lives.

Chapter 6

Fighting the Good Fight of Faith

Fulfilling your destiny and accomplishing your purpose are not easy. It requires commitment, dedication, common sense, and God's help. He tells us in 1 Timothy 6:12, *"Fight the good fight of faith, lay hold on eternal life, to which you are also called, and have professed a good profession before many witnesses"* (NKJ 2000). Once you discover your purpose, it will become easier, because when you are in your calling, it just fits, you feel it; you just know it down in your spirit. The challenges along the way, sometimes are those around you who become envious and even jealous because of your accomplishments (Song of Solomon 8:6). Sometimes, their resentment is so strong they are actually convinced they're justified in doing whatever is necessary to stop you. This deception becomes an instrument in the devil's hands to discourage you from doing what God has called you to do. You see, your calling makes you a specialist. When you are a specialist you become a target of the devil. Polling has shown that if just 10% more Christians in America would go vote, they could elect every office in the land from the White House to the local school boards, and everything in between. This is the kind of unity and power the devil hates!

As long as you are rocking along in the world and not seeking things of God, you are not a threat to the devil. It's only when you seek God's purpose for your life and influence others, that he takes notice. Then, when you really seek God for direction, specifically on how you can bring His Kingdom back to Earth, the devil will work overtime for your destruction (1 Peter 5:8). For example, the devil will put thoughts in your mind like, "you don't know what you are doing" or, "you are not worthy or even capable of accomplishing anything." Doubt, doubt, and more doubt, that is what he wants you to think. Remember, his goal is to defeat you. To combat this, you must put on the whole armor of God (Ephes. 6:11-18), and remember that your rear guard, *'prayer'* as a powerful weapon of choice. Intercessory prayer, individual prayer, and praying in agreement with others. When you enjoin your destiny and purpose with another's destiny and purpose you are not only formulating God's plan, you become a powerful force that the devil fears. The scripture is clear about the power of prayer, *"one will put one thousand to flight, but two will put ten thousand to flight"* (Leviticus 28:8; Deuteronomy 32:30, NKJ). In other words, you can be powerful when others pray with you, it's called "synergy," which is the interaction or cooperation of two or more organizations, substances, or individuals to produce a combined effect greater than the sum of their separate effects.

Even the world understands that being in agreement works. Although it is not prayer, the principles are similar. Successful businesses, for example, use the "Think Tank" approach where groups of employees meet together, isolate themselves in a room to share thoughts and ideas collectively, to formulate their goals for success. When you agree and pray together for God's purposes and seek His answers you push your prayer into the "Supernatural Realm." The reason for this greater power is revealed in Matthew 18:18-20 (NKJ), *"Where two or three have gathered together in My name, there I am in their midst."* The presence of Jesus can produce the answers to prayer. You only have to *"ask"* for His input (Matt. 7:7-12).

Whether you are seeking your purpose, your destiny, or already know God's plan for your life, you can never go wrong if you find God's direction before you act. Once you have God's heart about what you are asking and praying about you will seal your success. Matt. 18:19 says, *"Again I say unto you, that if two of you shall agree on earth as touching anything that they ask, it shall be done for them of my Father which is in heaven."* This verse is printed in Red ink. For those who may not know what Red ink means in the New Testament, these are words spoken by Jesus Himself. I pray quite a lot by myself, however when things aren't happening as often as it should, I get my wife to pray in agreement with me and the answers come! Sometimes, we may ask our son to join us in prayer, which makes us a *three-fold cord* that is not easily broken: Eccles. 4:12 (NKJ) - *"Though one may be overpowered by another, two can withstand him. And a threefold cord is not quickly broken."*

A great example of this was one Saturday afternoon in 2007, we were watching our son Cale, catch his baseball game, and I started feeling pressure in my chest. During his games, I always walked around or paced back and forth while watching him play or talked to the third-base coach between innings. Phyllis was sitting behind the back stop with a group of friends, but I did not say anything to her about the pressure in my chest, I just walked around trying to figure out what was happening to me. The pressure seemed to get worse, so I sat down at a picnic table. Phyllis glanced around and saw me sitting there and immediately came running over to me, asking, "What's wrong?" I said, "I think I am having a heart attack.'

She yelled for Cale (15 years old at the time), who had earned four certifications in EMT training as an Explorer, and also served as the Team Medical Assistant. He immediately pulled off his catcher's gear, grabbed his first aid medical bag from the dugout and came running, all while calling 911. Phyllis pulled the car around and they put me in the car with the seat reclined back. Cale popped an aspirin in my mouth and proceeded to give me a sternum rub. The paramedics arrived in record time, accessed the situation, put me in the ambulance and immediately hooked me up to a monitor. Cale wanted to ride with me in the ambulance, so Phyllis followed in our car. In the ambulance, the paramedics asked my son what he was seeing on the monitors? He told them the monitors are indicating that I was having a heart attack! They confirmed he was correct. Cale continued telling them about giving me the aspirin and doing a sternum rub, which they further confirmed was the right thing to do under the circumstances and congratulated him on a job well done. One of the Paramedics said, "Your quick-thinking efforts and cool head most likely saved your dad's life."

At Saint Joseph Medical Center emergency room, the doctors worked quickly to get an EKG, an ultra-sound, and an echocardiogram of my heart. The diagnosis was *atherosclerosis*, with 80% to 90% blocked arteries that would require four stents. They collected my prior medical history and called my previous cardiologist at Emory University Hospital. Dr. Walter remembered me well and talked at length with the attending cardiologist at St. Joseph Medical Center, Dr. Jack Chen. This time was totally different than the previous diagnosis of *arrhythmia*, which caused a complete heart block, and no medications were prescribed at that time.

The treatment for this latest heart episode, in addition to the stents, was 10 mg blood pressure medication and 325 mg aspirin daily. I could tell a big improvement of my energy level. The stents helped open up the blood flow and I was good to go until next year's annual check-up. A year later my check-up with my regular cardiologist, Dr. Shirazi, started out well; The doctor was even complimenting me on my "athletic heart" during the treadmill part of the stress test. However, upon resting afterward, with monitors still in place, it was discovered that my heart showed problems. I did excellent during the exercise portion of the test, but terrible in the resting state afterwards.

My cardiologist decided to put me in the hospital right away. Tests revealed a rupture of plaque which caused blockage and another mild heart attack. It was decided that I needed *quintuple bypass surgery* and my cardiologist started looking for a surgeon. Out of approximately four possible surgeons reviewing my past medical history, all turned me down except one; Dr. Gott, at Piedmont Hospital in Atlanta.

The surgery was set up early one morning in August of 2008. My wife, my son, my brother, and his wife, sat in the waiting room, praying for me while Dr. Gott performed open-heart surgery. Three and a half hours later, the doctor came out and spoke with my family and said, "All went well." Several years later, one of my doctors revealed to me that they almost lost me on the operating table, but he was able to stabilize me before any further damage was done. During this surgery a birth anomaly was discovered that had made my heart muscle weak and thin. In all probability, I have carried this heart problem since birth because I was born two months premature and weighed only two and a half pounds. Evidently, the devil has wanted to take me for a long time. This defect in my heart never showed up on any test before this open-heart surgery.

Dr. Gott had also decided to call for an implantable cardioverter defibrillator (ICD) to be installed inside my chest, a few days after the heart surgery. Dr. Prater, who was in the same group as Dr. Gott, was the cardiac-electro physiologist that implanted my defibrillator. This gadget prevents sudden death from cardiac arrest due to tachycardia, a life-threatening condition involving abnormal rapid heart rhythms. My ICD came with a bedside monitor as well.

When I finally came home from the hospital, I did very well, but I had contracted a staph infection in my left ankle where my veins were harvested for the bypass. From there, I developed blood poisoning and was given antibiotics to take for two weeks, which failed to clear up the infection. By phone, the medical team changed the antibiotic to something stronger, but it did not help either. A red streak was beginning to travel up my leg from the ankle, and I was running a very high fever. I had to check back into the hospital via the emergency room. Several more antibiotics were administered, and nothing worked.

One day, my assigned doctor was leaving my hospital room and a famous pathologist happened to be visiting the hospital on a different case from John's Hopkins Hospital in Baltimore. My doctor stopped him in the hall, shook his hand and took an opportunity to tell him about my situation and how no antibiotics were working to clear the infection spreading throughout my body. He came in my room, looked at my chart, and examined me. He wrote out a prescription for medicine that he referred to as "liquid gold" because it was so expensive. My doctor started me on an IV drip of this "liquid gold" antibiotic and before it was gone from the bag, my fever broke, and I was feeling great again!

Of course, Phyllis was praying and calling all her prayer warrior buddies to pray specifically on every single thing the devil would throw at us. I have so much to be thankful for, as well as blessed beyond words for my church, the many friends and faithful family members that prayed constantly for me. Sometimes it is over-whelming to think about how blessed I truly am. Miracles, miracles, and more miracles! Are you getting Gods message yet?

Many people who are going through all these things might say maybe it is time to retire. Honestly, I even thought about it myself, but the Holy Spirit quickly spoke to my spirit saying, " Mike, I am into 're-firing' not retiring." He then reminded me of a church service that we attended a few years ago at 'Life Center' in Dunwoody, Georgia. It's church leaders, Apostle Buddy and Prophetess Mary Crum called us out and prophesied to me, "Write the book." It was such a confirmation to what I knew in my spirit I should do. It sounded easy enough, but you would not believe the warfare I've experienced over writing this book. Yet, I knew that God would help me finish it, because this is part of my destiny.

Chapter 7

The Power of One

Now that you understand the importance of being properly covered in prayer, whether you are seeking to find your destiny and purpose or if you are wanting to expand your spiritual walk, there are some things that you can do to reclaim God's plan for mankind. The plan He meant for all of us from the moment He created heaven and earth.

In my testimony, I speak about the world systems or 'mountains' such as Government, Learning, Outreach, Business, Entertainment, Family, and Media. They are all in a mess. The world's approach to solving all their problems are not working and costs billions of dollars that never seem to make them better. These and many other world systems are failing. It is incumbent upon the Church, (not a denomination) but the Church Universal or the Bride of Christ to prepare itself by becoming expert in every way regarding world systems and how they work. As you think about how you will begin, do not allow the enemy to discourage you or convince you that you'll be wasting time because you are just <u>one</u> person, Remember, it only took one person to take prayer out of schools! You are important and have an essential role in God's overall plan. He needs you as part of the total picture. Unlike the world's approach, in God's plan, each role is important and each person as well as their assignment is as equal as the other. Scripture tells us, *"Submit yourselves therefore to God.*

Resist the devil, and he will flee from you." (James 4:7). Now kick the devils butt and get moving! Don't let him intimidate or control your life.

Here are some things you can do to get started:

1. Think about things that really appeal to you. Something that you can get passionate about.

2. Educate yourself on your chosen interests. Attend meetings. Find others with similar interests and talk with them about their ideas. Seek out ways to make your ideas heard, and do not get discouraged if your ideas are not readily accepted. Consider them as seeds planted.

3. Align yourself with a mentor or mentors that have the knowledge you need. Their experience will give you a wealth of information and will minimize your mistakes.

4. Be prepared for mistakes, even failures along the way. Accept your failures and learn from them.

5. Evaluate the causes of your mistake(s) and failures. Discuss them with your mentor(s) and make the necessary adjustments so that they will not be repeated.

6. Encourage yourself., like King David (1 Sam. 30:6 KJV). Be positive; stay focused on your purpose and destiny. There will always be the naysayers that will tell you all the reasons you cannot succeed.

7. Remind yourself daily that your purpose is an important part of God's purpose.

8. Pray daily that God will reveal to you ways to influence your surroundings, so His purposes can be fulfilled.

Influencing your surroundings can be a very delicate matter because you are interacting with a wide range of social, ethnic, and economic groups of people. It can be very intimidating. As you gain experience your confidence will grow as will your purpose. I remember the first time I walked into the Capitol and onto the floor of the Senate. There I stood, one of fifty-six senate members elected to lead the State of Georgia and its population of more than eight million people. I was humbled and honored to be in that position and immediately felt the weight of responsibility to the people who elected me to represent them back home in the senate district. Yet, before I had a chance to take everything in, the devil started on me with his mind games. "Well, you are here, and you do not have a clue how anything even works; What makes you think you are smart enough to be here?" Whenever these negative thoughts arise, block them out by thinking about something positive that has happened in your life. The Apostle Paul tells us, *"Finally, brothers and sisters, whatever is lovely, whatever is true, whatever noble, whatever is admirable ... if anything is excellent or praiseworthy ... think about such things and the God of peace will be with you"* (Philippians 4:8). For example, I am reminded of our son's Power of One praying and confessing a thing that came to pass.

As a young teenager, our son, Caleb, whom we and his friends sometimes called Cale, dreamed of having a K-9 search and rescue dog. After studying various breeds, he fell in love with the Belgium Malinois'. Cale was constantly watching YouTube videos of K-9 training camps in the US and Europe, studying various techniques such as bite work, search and rescue and drug interdiction. Back then, a purebred Belgian Malinois puppy cost at least $1,000.00, and the cost of training ranged between $35,000.00 - $100,00.00. Phyllis and I told him the only way he would get a dog like that was if God supernaturally placed one in his lap.

When Cale was 16, I received an invitation from Trinity Broadcasting Network (TBN) to appear on a live television show with Paul and Jan Crouch in their California studio. Our friends Kim and Jane Clement lived close by so we stayed a few extra days to visit with them. One evening after dinner, Cale went into the back yard to play with their dog, Henri, a highly trained protection K-9. Phyllis was sharing with Kim and Jane about how Cale was training a Labrador retriever back home to assist the local police department in search and rescue operations and how much he loved working with dogs. A few minutes passed, and Jane pushed back from the table, stood up, and said, "God spoke to me that I need to give Henri to Caleb." Then she ran outside to tell Cale.

I remember saying to Kim, "We can't let her do that." Kim said, "Leave her alone, I can tell you, this is God." As Jane approached Cale and Henri, she called them over and said to him, "How do you like your new dog?" Confused, Cale, said, "Ma'am?" And Jane replied, "I am giving Henri to you. He needs to be doing what you are doing in search and rescue work. He is bored and depressed here because he's not doing what he was trained to do." Cale was speechless. When she returned to the table, she explained what the Lord had told her to do. Phyllis and I were amazed and so thankful for their generosity of offering such a priceless dog to our son. Just then, Cale walked in with his laptop and pulled up his homepage where a Belgian Malinois appeared on the screen. the dog was an exact image of Henri, and the caption under the photo read: "This is my dream dog ... if I ever find him." What a miracle! Jane's obedience to God that day, placed a $35,000.00 dog in the lap of our son. What a faith builder for him!! Thanking God for something you don't even have yet will chase the devil away every time. This is faith, folks! And God responds to faith; He is not moved by tears, or begging, or assumptions. Faith. *"Now faith is the substance of things hoped for; the evidence of things not seen."* (Hebrews 11:1-6)

Never tell yourself, "I cannot do this. I don't know how." Yes, you can! Do not quit. Press yourself, think on things that are good. Speak it. You will find that you know more than you think, and you will grow into that specialist standing on the mountaintop as the one who has the ability to bring the right changes to your sphere of influence. Influencing your surroundings is just what you and God need to bring changes to our world systems. As you grow in knowledge and experience in your purpose and destiny, it becomes a force of accomplishment, and you will see that others within and outside your specialty will seek you out for solutions.

Congratulations! Your purpose and destiny have reached a new level of influence, and if used properly, there is no limit in how God can use you for His Glory.

Chapter 8

The Difference in 'the Gospel' and 'the Gospel of the Kingdom'

During my out-of body experience, it was revealed to me that there is a difference between "the Gospel" or the message of salvation that Jesus brought when He died on the cross at Calvary. Making atonement for all our sins, so that all are free from the Adamic curse. John 3:16 says it best, *"For God so loved the world, that He gave His only begotten son, that whosoever believeth in Him should not perish, but have everlasting life."* Because of this, if we believe, we are saved and restored to God, our Father. This is the basic message of salvation. My little grandchildren can quote this scripture and the two oldest (ages seven and eight) have accepted Jesus in their hearts and are filled with His Spirit. If you complain in their presence of any pain or sickness, they will immediately offer to come and anoint you with oil and pray for you. They have great faith.

If you read the Bible, especially the book of Matthew, you'll find Jesus Himself instructing His disciples not only to teach and/or preach "the Gospel," but the *"Gospel of the Kingdom"* to all the world. *"And this 'gospel of the kingdom' shall be preached in all the world for a witness unto all nations; and then shall the end come"* (Matt 24:14, KJV).

This message is for those who, after they receive salvation, and Christ lives in their hearts, the very things He did, you will do. Jesus said, *"Truly, truly, I say to you, he who believes in Me, the works that I do, he will do also; and greater works than these he will do because I go to the Father. Whatever you ask in my name, that will I do, so that the Father may be glorified in the Son. If you ask Me anything in My name, I will do it"* (John 14:12-14). Jesus did not remain on the cross! He took the keys of the Kingdom and went into hell and released all who had died before Him (Matt. 16:19). In addition, He didn't stop there, He ascended to the Father, where He now sits at His right hand making intercession for the saints (us)! We have both salvation *and* the power of the resurrection. He not only wants us to communicate this Gospel of the Kingdom, but to demonstrate it as well. As it says in Acts 14:22, *"Confirming the souls of the disciples, and exhorting them to continue in the faith, and that we must through much tribulation enter into the kingdom of God."*

So, what does this mean? This Kingdom I speak of is the government of God's rule that will forever exist after time has ceased. It is not limited to a heavenly realm, a geographic place, a race of people, or a nation on earth. The Kingdom of God is ruled by the King, Christ Jesus, not by outward disciplines, but *"peace, joy, and righteousness in the Holy Spirit"* (Romans 14:17). Those of us who submit our lives to the 'rule of Christ' will show forth these seeds and yield its fruit. God revealed to me that many know Jesus as Savior, but few yield to Him as Lord and King (Philippians 3:10).

The Church (Body of Christ) positioned in the world systems is like an 'embassy' of the government of God designated to bear witness to God's Kingdom; With an assignment to model or demonstrate the character, compassion, order, structure, and will of God's Kingdom on Earth as it is in Heaven. Therefore, the Church has a two-fold mission; 1) to preach salvation in Christ, and 2) to preach and demonstrate the Kingdom of God as a witness to influence the world. This proven standard working properly through His Church is the model in which God can judge the nations of the Earth.

We must have God-given strategies of how to address relevant issues within every kingdom (world system) of this world, in order to influence and reclaim them for God and His Christ. Without this, the enemy (devil) will continue to use his own evil system as he does to war against God's plan. Each of us has been given the *Keys of the Kingdom* (Matthew 16:19) to release people who are bound by satan's grasp and bring restoration to those trapped by sin and unbelief. Jesus made it clear that the end would not come until His people preach and witness the *Gospel of the Kingdom* (the rule of Christ) through demonstration and power in the Spirit, not just by persuasive words, to all nations (Matthew 24:14).

When my friend, Dr. Lance Wallnau, heard my testimony about my out-of-body experience, he was inspired by the revelation of the kingdoms of this world. The Holy Spirit gave him an interpretation of them as "Seven Mountains," that were named and to be conquered. He has spent years ministering and teaching this revelation to the church-at-large, as well as the world market places.

I was not called to preach or teach, I was called to write what I saw and heard in an out-of-body experience. I do not yet totally understand all that I was told by the Lord. I simply tell exactly what the Holy Spirit said and what I was shown in the brook. But I believe many leaders within the five-fold ministry will read this book and it will either confirm a thing already in their spirit or they will be inspired by the Holy Spirit with revelation knowledge and a word, lesson, or series will be birthed. If you don't understand something, don't worry, it's not time yet. God will give you understanding in due season according to His purpose for your life.

Jesus knew we would need help in order to accomplish all this, hence the reason He left us this very powerful "helper," called the Holy Spirit. He told His disciples in the book of Acts, chapter 1, verse 8 that "... *ye shall receive power, after that the Holy Ghost is come upon you: and ye shall be witnesses unto Me both in Jerusalem, and in all Judaea, and in Samaria, and unto the uttermost part of the earth."* This power was able to influence the whole world at that time and is the same power we have available to us today that helps us strategize the return of our King, Jesus. I believe we have truly entered into the last days, and His power is going to be poured out upon all flesh, young and old alike (Acts 2:17).

Let the Holy Spirit transform your life, your soul (which includes mind, emotions, will), and your spirit. (Romans 12:1-2). Become a 'Kingdom Shaker.' The Word of God says, *"Everything that can be shaken, will be shaken"* (Hebrews 12:27). But He has given us a Kingdom that cannot be shaken. This might sound like a contradiction, but one is referring to each kingdom or world system on earth (the kingdoms of this earth) and the other refers to the Kingdom of God in Heaven. The Word of God tells us, *"Jesus answered, my kingdom is not of this world: if My kingdom were of this world, then would My servants fight, that I should not be delivered to the Jews: but now is my kingdom not from hence"* (John 18:36).

I can boldly testify, not even death can shake His Kingdom, because the sin that once disrupted the tranquility of the Garden of Eden was restored by the shed blood of Jesus, the Lamb of God. The sons of the Kingdom, who have been planted within the world systems, will shine forth with the answers and solutions that are beyond the wisdom of this world (Romans 8: 19-22). When the Church has accomplished her faithful witness on earth, and God has destroyed all that is evil, then only Christ's righteous Kingdom will remain.

Chapter 9

Between Heaven and Earth

For years whenever I shared my personal testimony, I said that I was in this beautiful 'place,' but I never said where. I wasn't sure, but I always thought it was Heaven because it was so peaceful and magnificent.

In the summer of 2000, as Phyllis and I were driving back from a Florida vacation, she was reading to me from Prophet Kim Clement's book *Call Me Crazy, but I'm Hearing God.* In one chapter he wrote about the Garden of Eden and how it is still there, in a different dimension; exactly as it was when Adam and Eve walked with God. Kim pointed out in the scriptures that even after Adam and Eve were cast out of the Garden, He did not destroy it. Even the *Tree of Life* is still standing with the Cherubim guarding the entrance from every direction with a flaming sword! (Gen. 3:24.)

As I listened to Phyllis read, the Spirit of the Lord rushed through my body and chills ran over me from head to toe. I could feel the tears running down my face as she said to me, "Mike what's wrong?" I pulled the car over to the side of the road and, through my sobs I said, "After all this time, God just revealed to me where He took me during my out-of-body experience. I wasn't in Heaven, I was in the Garden of Eden!" I was overwhelmed to think that God took me to the place where He had walked and talked with Adam and Eve in the cool of the day, back before they sinned.

God revealed to me that He is restoring the 'Garden relationship' with man. What He had shown about the Garden of Eden was that *"Adam and Eve had to be sent out to work the ground from which he was taken. He drove out the man, and at the east of the garden of Eden he placed the cherubim and a flaming sword that turned every way to guard the way to the tree of life"* (Gen 3:23-24). The Tree of Life still remains but He could not allow Adam and Eve to have access after they disobeyed God and partook of the Tree of Knowledge of Good and Evil. This sin caused man to be sent out in case *"he reach out his hand and take also of the tree of Life and eat, and live forever"* (Gen 3:22b). Had Adam and Eve done so, they would have lived forever in a state of sin and separation from God!

But through the blood of Jesus Christ, we can partake of the Garden's fruits, because we have been restored to the Father. Some theologians believe that Noah's flood destroyed the Garden of Eden, but Revelation 2:7 says, *"He that hath an ear, let him hear what the Spirit saith unto the churches; To him that over-cometh will I give to eat of the tree of life, which is in the midst of the paradise of God."* Then in Rev.22:14 says, *"Blessed are they that do His commandments, that they may have the right to the tree of life and may enter in through the gates into the city."*

When you have an out-of-body experience, it tests the limits of your sanity. Questions come to you like, "Are you dreaming?" Or, "Is God bypassing my 'natural' understanding to show me something I could have never understood otherwise?" In the Gospel of Matthew 16:13-17, Jesus asked Peter, *"Who do men say I really am?"* Peter replied (paraphrased), *"Some say you're a lot of different things."* But Jesus asked Peter, *"Who do you say that I am?"* Peter answers, *"You are the Christ, the son of the Living God."* Jesus explained, *"you have by-passed your 'natural' mind (flesh and blood), Peter, and understood something no one else has understood yet (as God reveals)."*

I believe God took me to the Garden so I could understand a revelation and share it around the world. This information reveals how we can establish the Kingdom of God on Earth as it is in Heaven, or the Heavenly realm. We know from Matthew 24:14, that until the Gospel of the Kingdom has been communicated, Jesus is not coming back. And, the proof is in Rev. 11:15 (KJV) the demonstration of *"the kingdoms of this world are become the Kingdoms of our Lord, and of His Christ; and He shall reign forever and ever."* We have a work to do in helping with this!

As I tried to explain in my testimony, regarding my out-of-body experience, I could feel the glory and presence of the Lord everywhere and in everything. I truly understood the Scripture that talks about Him taking everything that is corruptible and making it perfect, along with *"this mortal has put on immortality ... death is swallowed up in victory!"* (I Cor. 15:53-54,

ESV). In the Garden, the sky was a radiant blue that was like nothing I had ever seen here on Earth. There was no smog or pollution, there was no trash or ugliness. Everything was pure, perfect and in order. There was no transportation, but I felt myself floating wherever I wanted to go. There was no need for words because it was like you could communicate the same way you do with the Holy Spirit now; in your inward man or spirit to Spirit. and the presence of Love in the atmosphere was so real, you could cut it with a knife! There was an overwhelming God-consciousness that enveloped my being and I found myself sitting down by a brook that ran through this beautiful garden. I sat down to talk with Him, my God, my Father, my Creator, in the cool of the day, just as Adam had done and it changed my life.

Gardens are special places. Adam and Eve were defeated in a Garden; Jesus defeated the devil in a Garden; Jesus rose from the grave in a Garden. Heaven's war room is a Garden. And I was there! You can make your home or your heart a garden, if you allow the Lord to come and fellowship with you and to show you His glory. We were created to have fellowship with God and to minister to Him. Many people minister to other people, but few know how or take the time to minister to Him. I am not sure if I am doing it correctly, but I am doing my best. The Garden is where the Presence of God came to fellowship with man. Try it, He will show up every time.

During my time of sitting and talking with the Lord, in the Garden, He spoke to me about His Glory.

Phyllis was especially interested in this because she had studied and prayed about the subject quite often. God simply showed me how 'we' produce His glory and it is very important to Him. The only place where God will manifest His power is in an atmosphere of glory. This is created by those that 'know' Him, or are intimate with Him, i.e., *"Adam "knew" Eve, his wife, and she conceived ... and she brought forth Cain"* (Gen. 4:4); In addition, we can praise Him with our lips, facing each other like the cherubim in Exodus 25: 20-22; *"And the cherubim's shall stretch forth their wings on high, covering the mercy seat with their wings, and their faces shall look one to another; toward the mercy seat shall the faces of the cherubim's be."* A secret of mercy and love that I learned is that we must worship God directly (vertically) and to one another (horizontally) for Him to show Himself in His fullness. That's why in church we praise in the congregation facing the choir or praise team. We produce His glory. God will move in between our faces and we will become the dwelling place of the Lord! Miracles happen in His Presence!

Back in Isaiah's time, in 2 Chron. 26, He recognized that he was an unclean vessel and felt unable to join in worship with the Seraphim, however his problem was solved when the angel purified his tongue with the coals from the *"altar of incense."* Today, we have the blood of Jesus that purifies every part of us! Now, we are called to be his vessels that fill the whole earth with His glory. Imagine the angels are in the heavenly dimension praising the Lord and speaking of the majesty of the Almighty God and we, as the body of Christ are worshipping toward heaven from the earthly dimension, what is happening in the midst of these two dimensions?! The miracles should be tremendous! I'm sure there are pockets of this happening from the earth, but nowhere near what it could be from the saints of God. I now cry out with the messengers of God for the earth to be filled with His glory. Jesus' recorded example prayer in Matthew 6:10 (KJV), *"Thy Kingdom come, thy will be done in earth as it is in Heaven."*

God is searching diligently for a people who will love Him, not for what He will give in return, but for Himself. *"For the eyes of the Lord run to and fro throughout the whole earth, to shew Himself strong on the behalf of them whose heart is perfect toward Him."* 2 Chron. 16:9 (KJV). Do not be afraid of the counterfeit spirits or copycat spirits from darkness, God will show you the truth. His desire is for you to be totally committed to Him. Jesus longs for us, His people, who are mature enough to know the difference between love and lust, a covenant relationship, not a pretentious Christian walk, the difference between spiritual gifts and exhibitionist-type human talent.

God said that He is gathering a remnant out of every nation and denomination, in the midst of a crooked and perverse generation, that will be His pure virgin Church, the Bride of Christ. In Revelation 22:17; the Spirit and the Bride cry out inviting this remnant to *"Come. And let him that is athirst come. ... let him take the water of life freely."*

Chapter 10

Restored

Once you've had a true encounter with God you can never go back to who you were before. If you try, there will be no life or anointing like in the *"old wine in new wine skins"* parable. Jesus said, "No one puts a piece of unshrunk cloth on an old garment; for the patch pulls away from the garment, and the tear is made worse. Nor do they put new wine into old wineskins, or else the wineskins break, the wine is spilled, and the wineskins are ruined. But they put new wine into new wineskins, and both are preserved" (Matt. 9:16-17, NKJ).

In this magnificent garden setting where I sat with the Holy Spirit, I could see the shadows of people on the horizon. There were mountains, hills, valleys, and a bright light like the sun was coming up. Revelation 1:16 came to my mind: *"His countenance was like the sun shining in its strength."* I was drawn to the light, but He said, "Be still. Sit and let me talk to you. Look in the brook."

With His voice He caused the rippling brook to become still; as smooth as glass. It was like a movie screen. I saw all the world's systems before me. I asked, "What does this mean?" He replied, "These are the kingdoms of the world. There are Christian people strategically placed in each of these kingdoms and He named seven, but there were more. Everyone is born with a purpose to take their positions and influence these kingdoms as witnesses." It was then that I understood my place in influencing the kingdom of government or politics.

Many Christians think the arena of politics is a corrupt and godless kingdom or system to be avoided at all cost. That is because the enemy has infiltrated and corrupted the kingdoms of this world. But our purpose is to reclaim them for our King. Believers who know Christ as the King of Kings also know we are called to take our places as royalty in the kingdoms of this world.

In my mind, one of the greatest politicians in the Bible was Moses. People were afraid of God's voice so, they appointed a man to hear from God for them. Moses spoke directly to God and vice-versa (Exodus 31:18). He also had the authority, prophetic strategy, clarity of mind, and spirit to go before the most powerful authority in the world in his day or time, Pharaoh. Moses influenced the most powerful 'kingdom of finance' of the known world at that time. The same is true with Joseph; who, not only strategically influenced the kingdom of finance and government in Egypt, he also influenced the kingdom of government in Israel. Could they be some of the prototypes of whom we should imitate today?

Jesus teaches us that everything in the Kingdom of God is about timing. We see Mordecai saying to Esther, *"God has brought you to the kingdom for such a time as this."* God has brought every one of you into the kingdom for such a time as this, in this 21st

Century. God has positioned you in one of the kingdoms of this world to help it become the kingdoms of our God.

King David was not anointed to be a priest, he was anointed to be a king. Think about that, a king is the ultimate politician. In the grand scheme of God's plan, I do not believe many people truly understand the great value that God places upon the earth, where the physical part of His creation has served its purpose and has become the 'stage' for Him to reveal His eternal purposes for the earth and all of creation. With the final judgment and removal of all wickedness, God will not destroy the earth, but will purify the heavens and the earth of all unrighteousness and cleanse it for the final habitation of glorified humanity. The earth will then become that Garden of Eden or Garden of the Lord without hostility or sin, where the righteous dwell in total security and spiritual rest with God. And finally, King Jesus and His Bride (the church) will reign together in His Kingdom; i.e., Heaven and Earth united in Glory with no separation, forever. This gave me great peace.

The Holy Spirit told me that I would not be able to stay there now, but I was going back to earth to accomplish my destiny. I remembered the Word of God tells us that Jesus has given us all authority in heaven and in earth. Jesus restored us totally to God! We were created in His image and that is not how we look, but we do have the ability to 'speak' like God when He said, "Let there be ... light!"

It says in Proverbs 18:21, *"Life and death are in the power of the tongue."* God spoke, and the worlds were formed. One of the gifts of the Spirit is *prophecy* (1 Cor. 12:8-10). Which means God speaking through men and women. There's power in our words. Jesus raised Lazarus from the dead with His voice (John 11: 38-44). He also cursed a fig tree with the same voice (Mark 11: 12-25). I know there are many sermons on these scriptures, but my point is that Jesus' voice or words spoke life and also spoke death. Our ability to speak life and death is the same, because Jesus restored all that was lost through Adam's sin on the Cross. When God can trust you with your words, then you will be able to speak life (and death).

In the Garden I said to the Holy Spirit, "please let me stay here and just bring my wife and son to me." I wasn't sure how much time had passed. It could have been 34 minutes or 34 years, but I believe it was similar to the experience Paul wrote about in his second letter to the Corinthians: *"I know a man in Christ who fourteen years ago - whether in the body I do not know, or out of the body I do not know, God knows - such a man was caught up to the third heaven"* (2 Cor, 12:2). The same thing happened to the Apostle John on the Isle of Patmos. John said in Revelation 1, *"I'm not sure if I was in the body or out of the body because I was caught up with the Lord."* It very well could be they both had visited the Garden of Eden like I did. The purpose of this encounter with God was Him wanting to show me what I was supposed to do on earth and what had been restored to all of us.

In order to further expound on this, I will need to repeat some things. As God was telling me all the things I was going to do when I went back to earth, my wife was holding my ankles while I was on the table in the emergency room. I had been legally pronounced dead for 34 minutes. Just when God had spoken these things into my spirit, the heart monitor began to beep. God had restarted my heart. Phyllis was speaking prophetically on earth calling me back, and from the Garden of Eden, l heard the word I needed to go back. In that moment, there was simultaneous unity between the two worlds. The Lord's prayer teaches us to pray, *"Thy Kingdom Come on Earth as it is in Heaven."* This sounds like a pretty good example to me.

Please know this testimony is not to make my wife or me a hero or to lift us up in any way. It's to assure you that we are all heroes of the faith if you simply use the authority God has given us. In the emergency room, the doctors and nurses were in disbelief and stunned at my wife's behavior. Most people are very surprised and uncomfortable when someone speaks with spiritual authority.

God wants to unify His will on earth as it is in Heaven in your life. When those two dimensions line up, the Garden of Eden relationship is in operation. Through intercessory prayer, we can reach into the heavenly realm and bring into the earthly realm the will of God and the things He declares is within our authority and dominion!

God gave Adam and Eve all authority and dominion in the Garden of Eden, this has been restored through Christ; dominion even over the weather elements. We need to understand this and take authority and dominion over the enemy and all that he thinks is still his. He was defeated at the cross!

We have more in Christ today than anyone ever had in the history of the Bible. We are overcomers of the world (1 John 5:3); false doctrines (1 John 4:1-4); the wicked one (1 John 2: 13-14); because of Jesus (Luke 11:21-22; John 16:32); Rev. 21:7 which says, *"He that overcometh shall inherit all things; and I will be his God, and he shall be My son."* We have been restored, walk in it, until Jesus returns! (Acts 3:21).

Chapter 11

The Open Door

The testimony of my miracle began to spread all around the world. Whether it was on television, in a church, or at a major Bible Conference, we began to tell the world about the miracle of being raised from the dead and my out-of-body experience. Every 'growth' season of my life since I was born, the enemy has tried to take my life. Every time the enemy has a test or strategy to destroy my destiny, the Holy Spirit opens a door. A new door ushers me into a different dimension in every area of my life. All of us have choices. The Bible refers to "doors" as being a way to choose. Revelation 3:8, "*... I set before you an open door, which no one can shut. For you have only a little strength, yet you have kept My word and have not denied My name.*" Adam and Eve chose the wrong door and it was an exit out of the Garden of Eden. Jesus came to earth and called Himself "the door." That door allows us to walk back into the 'Garden' relationship. I can tell you by the Spirit of God, I've seen that Garden and the reason I'm writing this book is there is a door that is opened before you today. It's a door that will take you to higher places you never thought possible.

The time you spend in the Garden, with the Lord, is where He begins to develop a different mentality in you. I call it the "garden mentality." A higher level of God-consciousness or awareness. Words are very important, especially if God is speaking them, even through a Prophet. The very reason that my wife knew it was not my appointed time to die, was that a Prophet had given us a 'word' about our future and she knew that we had not completed our purposes on Earth, therefore she was motivated to pray and call me back! Prophets can help you choose the 'right door' or 'confirm a thing' that God has spoken to your heart by giving a "Word from God' regarding your life.

After Phyllis called me back in that emergency room, we came home and started 'living' again, God spoke to her about fasting in a different way. He called her to a time or season of 'fasting her words.' This was because God had trusted her with the gift of faith. Not just a measure of faith or mustard-seed faith, but His faith! He would never take that gift back, so He had to show her how not to abuse this great gift. In fact, He told her that if she did not learn this quickly, it could require her life, if she misused it. In other words, He might take her home early, if she failed to obey Him and she cursed someone or something in error. Amazingly, she went to a higher level or dimension of compassion during this time, but it required a much stricter walk with God. Of course, this is her own personal testimony and maybe she will write a book one day, I can only tell you that her favorite scriptures during this time became Romans 12:1-2, "*I beseech you therefore, brethren, by the mercies of God, that ye present your bodies a living sacrifice, holy, acceptable unto God, which is your reasonable service. And be not conformed to this world: but be ye transformed by the renewing of your mind, that ye may prove what is that good, and acceptable, and perfect, will of God;"* and Philippians 3:10, *"That I may know him, and the power of his resurrection, and the fellowship of his sufferings, being made conformable unto his death."* At the end of this season of fasting her words, we had several personal prophecies from great men and women of God, but I only have permission to share this particular one that was taped and the last prophecy Kim Clement gave to my wife before he passed away;

""Phyllis, you are the breath behind this whole thing. I'm going to give you the honor that you deserve," says the Lord. It was your breath that raised a dead man up. It was your breath that brought life when everything seemed to be going wrong and just when the enemy said, "It's done, we've got them!" We got every time he said that about you. You breathe and your breath, which is in the Greek words "pneumo" (and I wrote them down because I wanted to share them with you, Phyllis, but maybe I can do it later, because I don't have it now). But the Greek words for it is "pneumo" and "Zoë pneumo", which means to breathe like God and to breathe with God. And then, because of you breathing in the same rhythm as God is breathing, you make alive. You make alive! That's what that word means. Succor. Succor is spirit of life; it makes alive."

""God says, "Your breath, and I'm talking about just your existence, just your presence and you don't even have to say a word (which is impossible). <laughter> But, just your presence, just your existence, just your life is a force that the enemy despises and

hates. Every time he thinks that he's got you down from a lie, an insult, or a verbal abuse, or someone saying something or belitterance (a belittling spirit) that's come from the church, God says, "Ignore it, it has never come from Me!" Just your breath will bring him (pointing to me) to the higher place. You brought him from the ground, you brought him from the bed, you brought him from the heavenlies ... him!"

"And God says, "but now it's time to go a little higher. It's time to go a little higher." God says, "In other words, I'm going to let you breathe out more, your words, your prayers, your very praise, your laughter, your negotiations, every part of it is what is going to bring you to the next level." And God says, "You're not ready for sickness; you're not ready for poverty. You are ready for the best years of your life!" And God says, "Just as your outfit is blue, so are the skies blue for you. Your best years ahead as you watch your son and you watch your husband," and now God says. "I'll place you there, but let Me give you the honor that is due you, says the Lord."

""YOU ARE MY FRIEND! And because of that, just like I went to Abraham when I was about to take Sodom and Gomorrah out and I went and stopped at his house and said, "Let us consult with Abraham, my friend forever, to see if I should do this thing. And, Abraham stood as a righteous one and said if there were just fifty, if there were just ten, and God said, "I listened to his heart and he sounded like me. And the reason that I like coming to your home and into your property is because I think you're just like Me, says the

Lord. You act like Me at times. You live like Me and when I come to you, you pray, and I hear Myself in you.""

""Listen, your property paid off! Quickly paid off! You don't have any debt! There's no debt, says the Lord. Because, what you're about to do is not regional, or even state-wide, but is an inter-national thing! Therefore, I anoint you through this prophet of God, as a couple; as one-voice, as three, a trilogy, a trilogy, a trilogy," says the Lord. A three-fold cord cannot be easily broken. You, your husband, and your son are the three-fold cord that I have put together with the Father, the Son, and the Holy Spirit." God says, "Together, we are going to do it. And this nation is about to end in this season of war and hatred and go into its greatest season!""

~Prophet Kim Clement~

When you've been in the "Garden atmosphere' you inhale the breath of God. When you've really been in the actual Garden, your presence and even your existence becomes a force that the enemy despises. When people attack you, and speak negative things about you, remember you just release God's breath and He will bring you to a higher place. This book introduces you to a "Garden Mentality" that is calling you to a higher place. Every time you pray in the spirit, your prayers become the breath of God. Every time you praise, your praise creates the atmosphere of God. Even your laughter and your business will be filled with the breath (pneumo) of God. I can tell you when you have a "Garden Mentality" even death has no effect on you.   Jesus said, *"These things I do, you will do, and greater things because I go to the Father"* (John 14:12). I wrote this book not, so you could marvel at my testimony, but so that you can enter into the Garden experience. Give no place to fear in your life. The Word says, *"God has not given you a spirit of fear, but of love, power, and a sound mind"* (2 Tim.1:7). Jesus is the ultimate door. John 10:9, "I am the door. If anyone enters by Me, he will be saved, and will go in and out and find pasture." May God bless you and give you courage to walk through every door that He opens to and for you.

Chapter 12

I'm Somewhere in the Future

The way God uses revelation and supernatural encounters, is that he uses a different emphasis and meaning of our testimony based upon the people to whom we are ministering. Even as I write this book, God is using different emphases about what happened to me. If I highlight any one part, it would take away from things that might stand out to some people but might not be important to others. Even though this testimony happened in the past, the principles are all about the future. The Kingdom of God is about the future.

Kim Clement wrote a musical chant in the prophetic that said, "I'm somewhere in the future, and I look much better than I look right now." As you walk in the perfect will of God, He shows you who you are in the future. It's like the spirit of Elisha; He knew what the enemy was going to do before the enemy planned his strategy. Proverbs 29:18 says, *"Where there is no vision, the people perish."* The opposite of this is also true. Elisha was a man who could envision his future. He served Elijah with great humility and his service so transformed him that several years after his death, his bones were still raising the dead and healing them! (2 Kings 13:21).

Jesus showed us how to "see" life and death with the cursing of the fig tree that was not bearing fruit. In John 12:24, *"... Unless a grain of wheat falls into the earth and dies, it remains by itself alone; but if it dies, it bears much fruit."* One may bear the outward indications of life, like the fig tree; it was green, but it was as good as dead as far as its destiny of reproduction. Unlike the green leaf, the seed is destined for productivity, therefore it must die, be buried, and resurrect in newness of life! Jesus 'saw' this fig tree in its greatest potential of unlimited reproduction and fulfillment of purpose; not just a beautiful green tree that was barren.

The Bible is full of principles and patterns. What God has shown me is that everything good or bad that happened to Jesus, had to do with 'our' future. God started reclaiming the whole Earth by putting a garden in the earth and then putting man in that garden. Salvation and healing were made possible by what Jesus did in the Garden of Gethsemane, not just the cross.

When Jesus said, *"Father, not My will but Your will be done."* (Luke 22:42; Matt. 26:39). He sealed our future and gave us life everlasting! Those 34 minutes I was dead was really when I became more alive than ever before. Those 34 minutes allowed me to see my future and God's purpose for me on earth.

Now I want you to take inventory of your life. What are you doing that is making a difference for the kingdom of God? The average person influences approximately 10,000 people during their lifetime. I encourage you, and I believe that God is instructing you, to make the kingdoms of this world the kingdoms of our God. How? By allowing Jesus to rule and reign in your life. And, *"allow your light to so shine among men that they will see your good works and glorify the Father in Heaven"* (Matt. 5:16). My good friend, Bishop Paul Lanier quoted this on Facebook that sums up my point perfectly, "When I am as obsessed with serving in the harvest as I am tasting the fruit of the blessing from the Garden; I will have both. However, until then I will have neither."

The Mount of Transfiguration was Jesus' way of showing that the Law (Moses) and the Prophets (Elijah) were fulfilled in <u>Him</u>. If Jesus brought salvation from sin to all mankind because of Adam's original sin, then He restored us to the Garden relationship with God at the cross. Symbolically, the appearance of Moses and Elijah represented the Law and the Prophets. However, God's voice from heaven, *"Listen to <u>Him</u>!"* clearly shows that the Law and the Prophets must give way to Jesus Christ, our Messiah alone (Matt. 17:1-3; 5-8). The One who is the future in a new and living way is not replacing the old, but is the 'fulfillment' of the Law. Grace now takes precedence over judgment. Countless prophecies in the Old Testament, and in His 'glorified form' saw a preview of His coming glorification and enthronement as King of kings and Lord of lords.

Finally, He told us at His resurrection, that we now have dominion and authority over all things in the earth now and in the future. The things He did, we would do and greater. Following Jesus' example, even Peter's shadow healed people (Acts 5:15-16), however Peter quickly gave glory to the name and blood of Jesus, not himself (Acts 3:12). The disciples proclaimed and demonstrated Kingdom authority as He had taught them to do. Philip, one of the first deacons, preached in Samaria. (Acts 8:12) ... *"But when they believed Philip as he preached the things concerning the Kingdom of God and the name of Jesus Christ, both men and women were baptized."* Are Christians trying to "take over?" Not at all. They are simply living as "light" and "salt" (Matt.5:13&14) to offer people a choice between the worldly standards and the covenants of God. I was told that you can tell if a man is truly 'broken in spirit' by his desire to be hidden from sight. No longer does he desire to receive any glory, but realizes his own humanity. He must remain transparent, however in order for the world to 'see' what true grace means in a person. Christians become witnesses in every world system to the standards of God's Word applied in every area of life. When this witness is complete, Christ will return and claim every earthly kingdom as His own and present them to God, the Father (1 Cor. 15:24).

Our prayer is that God will bless each and every one of you and we hope this book has inspired you to fulfill your purpose and destiny in this great experience called 'life.'

Meet the Author

Mike D. Crotts, former Senator from the State of Georgia, remains a rising star on the horizon of American politics and a major figure in God's newest effort to re-establish the moral vision of our society through Christian influence on its power structures. Mike continues to be a valuable resource to both the citizens and elected officials throughout Georgia and our nation. His tenure in public office while serving on prestigious and influential standing Senate committees such as Appropriations, Banking and Financial Institutions, Insurance and Labor, Reapportionment, Transportation, and Ethics established him as a highly-respected leader on both sides of the political spectrum; Mike spearheaded a number of important pieces of legislation which have become the benchmark for similar laws in other states.

In addition to his notable political career, Mike is a veteran of The United States Coast Guard. He is a very successful entrepreneur having earned the distinction of becoming the youngest real estate broker in the State of Georgia; obtaining his broker's license as a senior in high school. He is the owner of Crotts Realty Company; a Commercial Real Estate business. Further, Mike has been called to be a powerful voice in the church as he gives testimony to his miraculous return to life after death and an "out-of-body" experience following a sudden heart block in October 1990. Mike's return to life has also allowed him to enjoy family life with his wife Phyllis, son Caleb, Caleb's wife Kerri, along with four grandchildren. Together, they continue to serve the local church.

As you listen to him speak with characteristic confidence and humility, you will have little doubt that God has refined the talents and ambitions of Mike Crotts in the furnace of affliction and called him into the service of others as one of our brightest and most outstanding statesmen.

Mike and his wife, Phyllis are available to speak and share their testimony in conferences and churches in the United States and worldwide.

Visit us on the web at:

www.mikecrotts.com